GENESIS

A SELF-STUDY GUIDE

Irving L. Jensen

MOODY PRESS
CHICAGO

Contents

	Introduction	4
	Introductory Lesson	6
1.	The Book of Genesis	12
2.	Creation	18
3.	The Fall	26
4.	The Flood; Birth of Nations	33
5.	Abraham—Four Great Tests	40
6.	Abraham's God of Promise	46
7.	Abraham's Crucial Last Years; Isaac	57
8.	Jacob Striving for Blessing	64
9.	Jacob Learning True Blessing	71
10.	Joseph as Prisoner	79
11.	Joseph as Benefactor	85
12.	Joseph as Son and Brother	92
	Bibliography	99

Introduction

The book of Genesis is a message from God just as contemporary as it is important; for, among other things, it reveals the sources and causes of all that is achieved and experienced in the daily life of every human being.

It is earnestly hoped that this study manual will help the reader and student to see more clearly some of the beauties and wonders of this marvelous first book of the Bible and to appreciate the important relation that it bears to the other books of the Bible.

Incorporated in this self-study guide are various helps on analyzing the Bible chapter by chapter and paragraph by paragraph. Convinced that "the pencil is one of the best eyes," the writer has also given suggestions along the way on how the student may record his analyses on paper.

These lessons may be used either for individual Bible study or in classwork. When several are studying together, the chosen leader is a key to the success of the group study.

The following suggestions are directed especially to such leaders:

1. If any lesson seems too long for one meeting, undertake half the assigned work and leave the other half for the next meeting. Take no more than you can do thoroughly.

2. If possible, construct enlarged copies (made either on cloth or paper) of maps and charts for class use.

3. Insist that members of the class study the lesson at home and bring to the class written answers to the printed questions as far as possible.

4. Urge members to read the assigned chapters in the Bible first before they read the manual's comments. The recommended procedure is: (1) first read the chapters from the Bible; (2) then

try to write out answers to the printed questions; (3) last of all read the comments on the lesson.

5. Have a short review of the previous study at the beginning of each meeting.

6. Have one or more members of the class tell the story of each chapter or section briefly.

7. In tracing the journeys of Abraham, Jacob, and Joseph, a black tape or ribbon could be pinned on the map at the different places as each journey progresses.

8. Insist that the members of the class think and study for themselves. Give them opportunity to express their thoughts and the lessons learned. Refuse to lecture to the class.

Introductory Lesson

Bird's-Eye View of the Bible as a Whole

It is most important to have a clear conception of the Bible as a whole before taking up the study of a part. When we look at a picture or a landscape, we first let the eye sweep over the whole panorama, thus grasping at one glance the design of the whole. Afterward we consider it more attentively, dwelling on the details, noticing the mountain, the river, the valley, the field, each in its relative position. We thus obtain a more comprehensive and intelligent idea of the picture and are able to appreciate its meaning and beauty in a way that would not be possible if we had not seen it first as one great whole. The same thing is true in Bible study. Many people lack interest in the Bible because they have failed to see its plan, purpose, meaning, and beauty. Such failure often can be traced to studying disconnected portions of the Bible without seeing the relation of these portions to the whole.

If one keeps in mind the Bible as a whole, and the relation that each book, subject, or person bears to that whole, interest in the study will be enhanced manifold.

Let us then, in this lesson, look at the Bible as a whole before taking up the study of any part of it. We will consider its structure

STRUCTURE

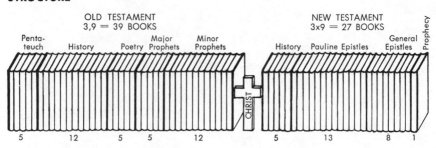

and history, its dispensations, and so forth, using charts as aids to memory.

1. *Number of books.* You will observe that the above chart represents the books of the Bible as separate volumes. To the left of *Christ* are the 39 books of the Old Testament, and to the right the 27 books of the New Testament. Look at that magnificent library. Sixty-six books in all, every one of them written by God and containing all that is essential for us to know. In them are found greater wisdom and knowledge than in all other books ever written in the history of mankind.

2. *Human writers.* No less than thirty-five men were employed in the writing of the Bible. God Himself is the Author of the Book, but He used different human writers to record His Word in written form. These "holy men of God" wrote as they were "moved by the Holy Ghost" (2 Peter 1:21*b*). They were men from every plane of life. Some were kings, some shepherds, some prophets, some soldiers, some fishermen. They lived in different ages—covering in all a period of sixteen centuries—and wrote in almost every conceivable form of literary style. Yet, when all their writings were brought into one volume, there were marvelous unity and harmony from beginning to end. This can be accounted for in only one way: there was one mastermind back of all. Every part of the total Scriptures was breathed out by one Person, God (2 Tim. 3:16-17).

3. *Literary style.* Notice the various kinds of literature in this sacred library. Here we have the finest law, the truest history, the most sublime poetry, the most marvelous prophecy, and the most instructive letters ever given to the human race. From a literary standpoint alone, the Bible is the Book of all books. The writer of Job is a far nobler poet than the writer Homer. The orations of Moses in the book of Deuteronomy far surpass any orations by Demosthenes or Burke. Science, discovery, and the excavation of buried cities are constantly confirming the absolute truth of the history contained in the Bible. We see before our eyes today the fulfillment of prophecies written here thousands of years ago.

How it must grieve God to see many people, even His redeemed children, ignoring this marvelous divine Book in favor of the uninspired writing of men.

Look at the preceding chart, and observe that there are five literary divisions in the Old Testament and four in the New Testament, marked off by heavy black lines, the names of the divisions being given at the top (Pentateuch, etc.), and the number of books in each division at the bottom of the chart. Learn the name of each division and the number of books it contains. The name "Pentateuch" means "five fold vessel" and refers to the five books of Moses. The designations "major" and "minor" for the prophets refer primarily to the length of the prophecies themselves. The number of Paul's epistles is fourteen if Paul wrote Hebrews. The General Epistles of the New Testament are so called because by and large they were intended to impart their message to various communities of Christians rather than to any particular individual or church.

HISTORY

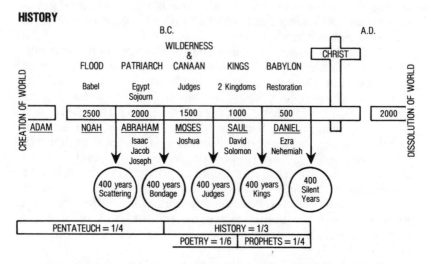

The main events and periods of Old Testament history are shown on the accompanying chart, located according to approximate dates. The Bible text does not record dates as such, but it does furnish data (e.g., relating an event to the "nth" year of the king's reign) from which many dates can be derived. God has hid from us the date of the future dissolution of this earth (see 2 Pet. 3:10-11), even as He has done with the date of its creation. It must also be recognized that the date of the creation of man is very difficult to determine from any source. It is a noteworthy fact in this connection that no evidence of civilization has ever been found antedating, at the earliest, 10,000 B.C.

Notice the five periods of 400 years, which occur at regular intervals. (In most cases the 400 is a round number.) Next fix in your mind the names (underlined) and dates of the key persons preceding each 400-year period. (Other important persons are identified below the underlined names, such as Isaac, Jacob, and Joseph.) Finally, associate the principal historical events with the persons and periods:

8

(1) Events from Noah to Abraham Wickedness of the World Great Flood Building of Babel	(3) Events from Moses to Saul Wilderness Journey Conquest of Canaan Leadership of Judges	(5) Events from Daniel on Captivity in Babylon Restoration of the Jews
(2) Events from Abraham to Moses Journeyings of the Patriarchs Sojourn in Egypt	(4) Events from Saul to Daniel Reign of Kings Two Kingdoms (Israel and Judah)	

The New Testament furnishes history only for the first century A.D. Some of it prophesies the spiritual conditions of the centuries after the first; most of its prophecy describes the events of the last days without furnishing any dates.

As for Old Testament history, notice what areas of historical record are furnished by each of the four sections of the Old Testament, namely, Pentateuch, History, Poetry, and Prophets (see bottom of chart). The fractions represent quantitatively the fractional part of each section in the entire Old Testament. For example, the prophets, whose pages add up to about one fourth of the entire Old Testament, cover a relatively short period of history, whereas the Pentateuch, of the same length as the Prophets, covers the longest period of history.

On the adjacent chart the space to the left of the cross is B.C., and the space to the right A.D. The first semicircle represents that far-off eternity before the world was inhabited by man; the last semicircle the eternity of the future.

DISPENSATIONS

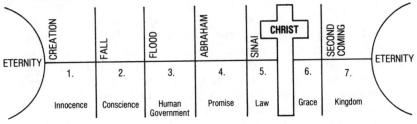

A. *Definition.* The term "dispensation" is used to designate a period of time during which (1) God's progressive revelation to man, (2) His sovereign will manifested in history, and (3) man's response to God's revelation, when combined in a composite picture, represent a distinct era in the history of mankind. Some dis-

9

pensations are short, others long. Bible history does not explicitly identify the commencement of every new dispensation. However, the sequence of seven dispensations is clear from a study of Bible history.

B. *The Seven Dispensations.*
    1. The Dispensation of *Innocence*, extending from the creation to the Fall. Adam and Even knew no sin until the Fall.
    2. The Dispensation of *Conscience*, extending from the Fall to the Flood. In the absence of a written law, the human heart reacted to the voice of God speaking to it, its conscience sitting in judgment on the decisions.
    3. The Dispensation of *Human Government*, extending from the Flood to Abraham. God gave directions to live by, but man chose to go his own way (e.g., tower of Babel).
    4. The Dispensation of *Promise,* extending from Abraham to Sinai.
    5. The Dispensation of *Law*, extending from Sinai to Christ.
    6. The Dispensation of *Grace*, extending from the Cross to Christ's second coming.
    7. The Dispensation of the *Kingdom*, extending from Christ's second coming to the end of world history. This is the millennial kingdom on earth. The first five dispensations have passed, and we are living in the sixth, the Dispensation of Grace. The titles of the dispensations should not be misunderstood to suggest any exclusiveness of God's workings, as though, for example, God did not manifest His grace in the Dispensation of Law, or that His law is not applicable in the present dispensation.
    The first three dispensations, Innocence, Conscience, and Human Government, recorded in the first eleven chapters of Genesis, cover a period of several thousand years. During these years, from Adam to Abraham, we have the record of God's testing of the whole human race. The next two dispensations, Promise and Law, recorded in the rest of the Old Testament, cover a period of two thousand years and record God's calling out the one nation of Israel. The sixth dispensation, Grace, has already extended nearly two thousand years during which time God has been calling men to repentance and faith in Christ Jesus.
    A careful study of these dispensations will reveal that each one begins with a fresh revelation of God's will and a specific command given. The first three very definitely end in failure, with the human race going its own way, independent of God. Each of the last four is part of the design of God to bring to the world a Saviour, the Messiah. In the Dispensation of Promise the nation

through whom He would come to the world is promised blessing. In the Dispensation of Law the individuals of the nation are shown their need of a Saviour by the very fact that they cannot keep the law. In the Dispensation of Grace the Saviour appears, in the flesh, to bring the offer of salvation to all the world. In the last dispensation the Messiah reigns over the kingdom, the ultimate fulfillment of the promises of the fourth dispensation.

1. Innocence	Command, Genesis 2:16-17	Failure, Genesis 3:6
2. Conscience	Command, Genesis 4:7	Failure, Genesis 6:5,11-12
3. Human Government	Command, Genesis 9:1-7	Failure, Genesis 11:1-4
4. Promise	Command, Genesis 12:1-3	Emphasis on Faith
5. Law	Command, Exodus 19:5-6	Emphasis on Obedience
6. Grace	Command, Acts 16:31; Mark 16:15	Emphasis on Faith and Witness
7. Kingdom	Revelation 20:4	Church Reigning with Christ

The Dispensation of Grace has not ended yet, but daily its history is fulfilling the Bible's prophecies. The church would do well to look back on history and ask herself a question: Is the church carrying out God's revealed will for these last days? It is almost two thousand years since Christ said to His followers, "Go therefore and make disciples of all the nations" (Matthew 28:19). Reports of world-wide distribution of translated Scriptures today are exciting. As of 1989 the 1,907 languages into which at least one book of the Bible has been translated represent approximately 98 percent of the world's population. This means that portions of Scripture are *accessible* to the large masses of the world in their native tongues. Such a report is encouraging, but it is also a challenge and a renewed appeal to all Christians to be faithful servants of the Lord of the harvest, praying and working until He returns.

Lesson 1
The Book of Genesis

The study of the Bible by individual books is as important as it is fascinating. As we enter into the study of any book of the Bible, questions such as these should come to our minds at the very outset: What is the object of this book? What is its chief theme? Who wrote it? When was it written? How long a period of time does it cover? What relation does it bear to the Bible as a whole, and to the other books of the Bible? In the study of Genesis, answers to some of these questions will be found in the biblical text itself. The other questions are answered in the later comments of this lesson.

GUIDES AND HELPS FOR A SURVEY STUDY OF GENESIS

This is the time in one's study for the "skyscraper" or overview survey of the book of Genesis. Leaf through the book first for casual observations, reading such things as (1) the first and last verses of each chapter, (2) headings at the top of the pages of your Bible indicating general contents, and (3) headings at the beginning of each chapter. In this process also your eye will fall upon different verses now and then that will give you the feel of the book you are studying. Now take a sheet of paper and list the numbers one through fifty (each representing a chapter of Genesis). For each chapter write down a word or phrase that would represent or suggest something of the contents of that chapter. Choose picturesque words, if possible. At times you may have to read a substantial portion of the chapter itself to get such a chapter title. After doing this for all fifty chapters, you will have a better grasp of the topics covered by the Genesis account.

Now try to answer these questions:

1. Contrast the first and last chapters of Genesis. Genesis goes from where to where?

_____

_____

2. In what chapter do the first names of the human race appear?

_____

3. Name some of the major *characters* of Genesis.

_____

_____

4. Name some of the major *events* of Genesis.

_____

_____

_____

5. From the events themselves, what do we learn of God? Of man?

_____

_____

You have been on your own in the study thus far. Now read the remainder of this lesson for further suggestions. Look up references whenever they are given.

I. *Name.* Genesis is the book of beginnings, as the word indicates. This word describes the relation that Genesis bears to the rest of the Bible. "Here in direct statement, or illustration, or type, all things material or moral are traced to their origin." Genesis has been called the "seed book of the Bible," the rest of the Bible just a blossoming out of the seed truths found there. Hence the importance of the book of Genesis.

Some of the great beginnings in Genesis are:

1. the beginning of the created universe (Gen. 1:1)
2. the beginning of man (Gen. 1:27)
3. the beginning of the sabbath (Gen. 2:2-3)
4. the beginning of marriage (Gen. 2:22-24)
5. the beginning of sin (Gen. 3:6; cf. Gen. 2:16-17; 1 John 3:4)
6. the beginning of sacrifice or salvation (Gen. 3:21; cf. Isa. 61:10; Gen. 3:15)
7. the beginning of prophecy (Gen. 3:15)
8. the beginning of human government (Gen. 9:1-6)
9. the beginning of nations (Gen. 11)

10. the beginning of Israel, the chosen nation (Gen. 12:1-3).

In these days there are many theories as to the beginning of the universe, man, sin, nations, and so forth, but in Genesis we have God's account of their origin.

II. *The Structure of Genesis.* Use the accompanying chart of Genesis for a survey of its major structure, noting the following points:

GENESIS BOOK OF BEGINNINGS

CREATION	FALL		FLOOD	BIRTH of NATIONS	ABRAHAM	ISAAC	JACOB	JOSEPH

25:19

1/2/3/4/5/6/7/8/9/10/11/ 12/13-23/24/25/26/27/28-35/36/37/38-49/50/

OVER ←2000 YEARS→ THE RACE AS A WHOLE	←300 YEARS→ THE FAMILY OF ABRAHAM
EVENTS PREDOMINANT	PERSONS PREDOMINANT

1. Genesis has fifty chapters. Most of the numbered spaces in the accompanying chart represent a chapter each. Draw your own chart and fill in a title for each chapter.

2. The first eleven chapters of the book cover a period of a few millennia and give the history of the human race from Adam to Abraham (see history chart, p. 8). This period includes the first three dispensations of Innocence, Conscience, and Human Government (see chart of dispensations, p. 9).

3. Chapters 12 to 50 cover a period of about three hundred years and record the history of four of the great men of the nation of Israel, that is, Abraham, Isaac, Jacob, and Joseph.

4. Observe that there are two main sections in Genesis, the first dealing with the race as a whole (chaps. 1-11) and the second

dealing with the family of Abraham (chaps. 12-50). In the first section, *events* are the key subjects to remember. They are the creation, Fall, Flood, birth of nations. In the second section, *persons* are the key subjects to remember. They are Abraham, Isaac, Jacob, Joseph. Learn the general chapter outline for these eight subjects. (Chap. 5, omitted from this outline, serves as a connector between the stories of the Fall and the Flood. Also note from the chart that the biographies of Abraham and Isaac meet in the middle of chap. 25.)

Events	Chapters	Persons	Chapters
1. Creation	1-2	5. Abraham	12-25
2. Fall	3-4	6. Isaac	25-26
3. Flood	6-9	7. Jacob	27-36
4. Nations	10-11	8. Joseph	37-50

III. *Writer.* Jewish tradition ascribes authorship of the first five books of the Bible to Moses. Christ explicitly ascribes the Pentateuch to Moses (Luke 24:44). The Jews divided the Old Testament into three parts: the Law, the Prophets, and the Writings. See also how Christ frequently referred to different books as being written by Moses. (Cf. Matt. 8:3-4 with Lev. 14:3-4; Mark 12:26 with Ex. 3:26; Matt. 19:7-8 with Deut. 24:1-4).

IV. *Date.* Moses probably wrote Genesis during the latter half of the fifteenth century B.C. This date is based on two assumptions: (1) that he wrote the book after the Exodus from Egypt, and (2) that the Exodus took place around 1445 B.C.

V. *Geography.* In the first eleven chapters of Genesis, which record the history of the human race for the first two thousand years, the geographical location of places mentioned is not well defined; but beginning with the life of Abraham in chapter 12, every place mentioned should be located on the map (pp. 48-49). Do not neglect this. It will greatly enhance your interest in Bible study.

VI. *Prophecies.* There are three distinct prophecies of Christ in Genesis. They are as follows:

1. The Seed of the Woman (Gen. 3:15)
2. The Seed of Abraham (Gen. 12:3)
3. The Seed of Judah (Gen. 49:10)

Observe that the first of these prophecies is general. It simply states that the coming Saviour of the world was to belong to the human family. The third prophecy is more explicit and points out the tribe from which Christ was to come. As we read on through the other books of the Old Testament, other prophecies tell the details of Christ's person and work so minutely that when Christ came and fulfilled exactly all these prophecies, there was absolutely no excuse for failing to recognize Him as the Saviour, promised from the day sin entered the world.

VII. *Types of Christ.* "A type is a divinely purposed illustration of some truth. It may be (1) a person (Rom. 5:14); (2) an event (1 Cor. 10:11); (3) a thing (Heb. 10:20); (4) an institution (Heb. 9:11); (5) a ceremonial (1 Cor. 5:7). Types occur most frequently in the Pentateuch, but are found, more sparingly, elsewhere. The antitype, or fulfillment of the type, is found usually in the New Testament" (C.I. Scofield).

SOME OF THE GREAT TYPES IN GENESIS

Things as Types	Persons as Types
1. Light	1. Adam
2. Coats of skin	2. Melchizedek
3. Ark	3. Isaac
4. Ladder	4. Joseph

VIII. *Progressive revelation in Genesis.* The Bible as one book is a progressive revelation, each book taking the reader one step further in the unfolding of God's character, His plans and purposes, His will and desires. Likewise, within each book of the Bible is a progressive revelation. Refer to the chart of Genesis, page 14. The eight main subjects of the book indicate a progression in the revelation of God's attributes, thus:

Creation. Chapters 1 and 2 reveal to us the *power* and *wisdom* of God. If we knew nothing of Him except what we learn in these first two chapters, we would know He is all-powerful and all-wise to create this universe and so marvelously fit this world for the habitation of man (cf. Ps. 19:1-6).

Fall. Chapters 3 and 4 reveal to us the *love* and *mercy* of God who, when the human race disobeyed His command and rebelled against His sovereignty, came seeking them and provided a way by which they could regain their lost estate.

Flood. Chapters 6 to 9 reveal the *justice* and *holiness* of God. Sin is abhorrent to Him. He is of purer eyes than to behold sin. He must punish sin.

Nations. Chapters 10 and 11 reveal the *sovereignty* of God. He is King. He rules the world. He has power over all mankind. He will be obeyed.

Abraham's life. Chapters 12 to 25 show forth God as *Saviour*, unfolding His redemptive plan in the creation of an elect nation.

Isaac's life. Chapters 25 and 26 show forth God's *faithfulness*, in the fulfillments during Isaac's life of His promises concerning Israel.

16

Jacob's life. Chapters 27 to 36 show forth God's *grace*, His "unmerited favor." Jacob did not merit any favor from God. He had no claim, either by right of birth or character, to the blessings he received, yet all through his life God showered him with blessings.

Joseph's life. Chapters 37 to 50 show the *providence* of God, how He watches over His own, guards them from evil, makes all things work together for good to them that love Him. He manipulates everything, making the most likely and the most unlikely circumstances minister to the working out of His great purposes for His people.

SUMMARY

The survey study of Genesis unfolds truths just as interesting as they are grand. Some of the more prominent ones are:

1. A *contrast*: the impersonal record of the divine creation of the universe and the personal record of the parents of the human race and their sin.

2. A *progression:* a progressive revelation of the nature of God.

3. A *particularization:* describing first the race as a whole, then the chosen family of Abraham.

4. A *projection*: the beginnings of things, peoples, behaviors, and so on, with prophecies as to the future outcomes.

Lesson 2

Creation

The first thing to do is to read carefully, prayerfully, and repeatedly the two Genesis chapters of this lesson in order to become acquainted with not only the facts of the account but how the facts are woven together into a complete record. It will help you immeasurably if you record briefly the main content of each paragraph on rectangular charts (such as those below), using the paragraph divisions suggested herewith (we might call these "analytical" charts to differentiate them from the survey charts, e.g., that of Genesis, Lesson 1):

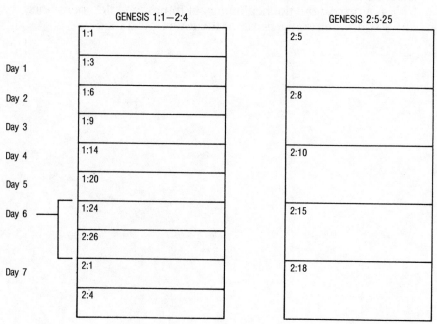

GENESIS 1:1—2:4

GENESIS 2:5-25

	1:1
Day 1	1:3
Day 2	1:6
Day 3	1:9
Day 4	1:14
Day 5	1:20
Day 6	1:24
	2:26
Day 7	2:1
	2:4

2:5

2:8

2:10

2:15

2:18

On these rectangular charts you will want to record not only isolated facts but related facts, including groupings. After you have jotted down such observations, try to answer the following questions:

1. Is there an introductory and concluding statement to the Genesis creation story? If so, where?

_____

_____

2. How is the account of 2:4b-25 related to the section preceding it? Does it continue the story? Expand on it? Give an alternate reading? Amplify one part of it?

_____

_____

3. Is there any order in the day-to-day creation series? What is the climax of the series?

_____

_____

4. What lessons do you learn from the program of the seventh day?

_____

_____

5. Make a study of names in these two chapters.

_____

_____

6. Notice how early in the Bible the first "thou shalt not" appears. What is God's motive in such prohibitions?

_____

_____

7. Was Adam without a wife for very long? What may one conclude about the husband-wife relationship from this account?

_____

_____

8. Write down any questions you have concerning these two chapters, and attempt to answer them after you have finished this lesson.

_____

_____

9. What is the main intent of the Bible's creation account?

_____

_____

10. What do these chapters teach about God?

_____

_____

11. What do these chapters teach about man?

_____

_____

I. THE ORIGINAL CREATION (1:1-2)

The book of beginnings starts with the creation of the unformed universe, and the author accounts for it in one sentence: "In the beginning God created the heaven and the earth." He says nothing as to the details of how or when but just that in the far-off beginning, however remote that may be, God created *all* things.

Some hold that after the original creation of verse 1 there was a pre-Adamic catastrophe plunging the world into the condition of chaos described in verse 2. If such was the case, the time interval between the two verses could be millions of years long, accounting for whatever are the geologic ages of the earth's history. The other view is that verse 2 describes not disorderly chaos but an unformed mass of material, which God then proceeded to take and form on the creative days according to the predetermined design. The Bible student's attention must be directed primarily to what the Bible says, not to what it does not say. Because most of chapter 1 is devoted to describing God's activity on the six creative days, it is obvious that *this* is the creation (whether or not there was an earlier creation) that is of paramount importance to the Bible student. In this creation record we have the story of God's preparing the earth to be the dwelling place of the human race and, when all was in readiness, of God's creating man and putting him there to glorify his Maker.

The account of 2:4b-25 is interpreted by many liberals to be a second creation story, written by a second author, since it contains references to God's creation already recorded in chapter 1 (cf. 2:19). But let us compare the two sections, and from our observations make a fair conclusion.

Chapter 1 records in *brief outline* God's creative work with reference to the universe and the world. We are told briefly what He did on the first day, the second, the third, the fourth, the fifth, and the sixth. But the Bible is not a history of the universe. It is the history of man, especially the redemption of man. Therefore, in chapter 2 God tells us in detail about the creation of man, explains his nature, surroundings, obligations, and so forth. Whenever Moses restates items of the chapter 1 story in chapter 2, he is doing so only to give context to what he is saying about man. So we have in these two chapters not two *differing* accounts of creation but creation in outline in chapter 1 and creation of man in detail in chapter 2.

II. THE SIX DAYS AND THE SEVENTH (1:3–2:3)

Let us notice the order of events on these six great days as though we were watching the transformation taking place before our very eyes. First, we see the earth, which was without form and void, and the Spirit of God brooding over it, as though He were looking out over the vast expanse, meditating.

On the *first day* God said, "Let there be light," and instantly there was light. The light was separated from the darkness. God called the former Day; the latter He called Night.

On the *second day* God formed the firmament, the great expanse dividing waters that were above it from waters under it. The expanse He called Heaven.

On the *third day* there was a gathering together of the waters under the heavenly expanse into what God called Seas, and the dry land—which He called Earth—appeared, forming the continents and islands. Soon afterward green grass and trees were made to appear.

On the *fourth day* the lights in the firmament of heaven, that is, the sun, moon, and stars, were made to function.

Verses 14 through 18 do not necessarily teach the original appearance of the luminaries. The sun and moon might have been created on the first day, being the source of the light of the first day (v. 3-5). The Hebrew word translated "made" in verse 16 ("And God made two great lights") is intended here to mean "appoint for a function." The same Hebrew word is used in Deuteronomy 21:12 (*"pare* her nails") and 2 Samuel 19:24 (*"trimmed* his beard").

On the *fifth day* God created fish in the water and fowl in the air.

Then on the *sixth day* the cattle, the creepers, and the beasts of the field were created, followed by the last and greatest of all —man, male and female. Just here, in this outline chapter, we are not told how the male and female were created. These details are reserved for chapter 2. Here we are simply told that God created man in His own image, male and female created He them, and gave them dominion over the whole earth (vv. 27-28).

The *seventh day* was an integral part of the creation week. It was not appended to the six days because God was tired. The *rest* of God was a ceasing from the creative activity ("he rested ... from all his work," 2:2). The seventh day was given a unique status among the days of the week, marked by four *principles* that would carry over even into the Church age's "first day":

1. The principle of *completion.* The day marked the successful completion of the total creative work. "God ended his work." The Christian's "Lord's day" especially witnesses to this principle, in God's acceptance of the Son's finished redemptive work by raising Him from the dead on the first day of the week.

2. The principle of *ceasing.* Man was inherently made with the requirement of periodic inactivity for spiritual, mental, and physical health.

3. The principle of *blessedness.* God's joy was in the creation of all that was *good* (1:31). The Christian's joy is in God his Lord.

4. The principle of *holiness.* God sanctified the day (2:3) in the sense that He set it apart from the others. The Lord's day for the Christian is intended so to be set apart from the other days in its program.

III. THE CREATION OF MAN (2:4-25)

In chapter 2 let us consider carefully this being—man—to whom God gave dominion over the works of His hands. Let us notice with what nature he was created, what his surroundings were, what was expected of him, so that we may better understand all that follows in the next chapters.

1. *Man's nature.* Verse 7 clearly states that man was created by God. In that original creation he was not made an inanimate object; the "breath of life" was "breathed" into him, and he "became a living soul." That he was also created with a spirit is demanded by 1:27, which tells us that "God created man *in his own*

22

image." We learn from 1 Thessalonians 5:23 that man has a body, a soul, and a spirit. Spirit gives man God-consciousness, enabling him to hear God's voice and respond to Him. Soul implies self-conscious life, including abilities such as reasoning. The animals have body and (in the sense of self-conscious life) soul, "but the highest beast has no trace of God-consciousness—the religious nature." Between animal life and human life there is a great gulf—a fixed gulf.

2. *Man's original habitat* (vv. 8-14). God expressly arranged a most beautiful garden in Eden to be man's home and surrounded him with everything to make him happy. (Make a list of good things identified with this environment.) Eden was probably located in the vicinity of ancient Mesopotamia (modern Iraq). In the days of Adam a river originated in Eden, watering Adam's garden, then parting into four branches: Pison, Gihon, Hiddekel (Tigris), and Euphrates. (The location of the first two rivers is unknown to us.) It is well for us to recognize that the topography of Adam's day was not exactly the topography of today, if for no other reason then the desolations of the Noahic Flood.

3. *Man's moral testing* (vv. 15-17). Being created with the power of choice, some tests had to be given Adam to prove whether he would choose to obey or disobey God. The test selected was neither ambiguous nor severe—Adam was commanded to refrain from eating the fruit of a certain tree in this garden. God not only gave the command but took pains to explain to the man why he must not disobey: "In the day that thou eatest thereof thou shalt surely die."

4. *The helpmeet given man* (vv. 18-25). The Lord said, "It is not good that the man should be alone; I will make him an help meet for him." Before making this helpmeet God caused all the beasts of the field, which He had formed out of the ground, to pass before Adam. Adam looked at them and gave them names, thereby showing that he was from the very first a highly intelligent being with the power of speech. But the animals afforded no suitable companionship for Adam, for they were not of the order of spiritual beings, as Adam. So God created such a helpmeet. He "caused a deep sleep to fall upon Adam . . . ; and he took one of his ribs, and closed up the flesh . . . ; and the rib, which the Lord God had taken from man, made he a woman, and brought her unto the man." The creation of Eve from a rib was no less a miraculous work of God than the creation of Adam from earthly dust. Any objections to such miracles reveal doubt and disbelief, not faith. For it is by faith that we can understand the coming into being of things visible and things invisible (Heb. 11:3).

The human pair of man and wife is now different from all other pairs; they are one. Paul shows how beautifully this creation of the woman typifies the church of Christ (1 Tim. 2:13; Eph. 5:28-33).

What a bright picture these first two chapters of the Bible present. Unfallen man, surrounded by everything to make him happy, had only one command laid upon him to test whether he would take his proper place as a creature subordinate to his Maker.

F.B. Meyer has beautifully written, "Man was placed in the world like a king in a palace stored with all to please him, monarch and sovereign of all the lower orders of creation. The sun to labor for him like a very Hercules; the moon to light his nights, or lead the waters around the earth in tides, cleansing its shores; elements of nature to be his slaves and messengers; flowers to scent his pathway; fruit to please his taste; birds to sing for him; beasts to toil for him and carry him; and man himself, amid all this luxury, as God's representative, God's vice-agent. This is man as God made him. We see him now as sin has made him. His crown is rolled in the dust and tarnished. His sovereignty is strongly disputed by the lower orders of creation. The earth supplies him with food only after arduous toil. The beasts serve him only after they have been laboriously tamed and trained, while vast numbers roam the forests, setting him at defiance. So degraded has man become through sin, that he has bowed before the objects that he was to command, and has prostrated his royal form at shrines dedicated to birds, and four-footed beasts, and creeping things."

This is as sin has made him. But it was not so from the first. If we would see man as God intended him to be, we must go back to Eden, see him as he came from the hand of God, pure, intellectual, kingly, godlike.

IV. SOME FINAL CONSIDERATIONS

Before leaving the consideration of these first two chapters of Genesis, notice a few points:

1. The entire human race has descended from one original created pair. The *unity* of the human race is of far greater theological import than the *antiquity* of the human race.

2. Some ask, "Were the days and years in the beginning of human history the same as now?" Regarding this, see Genesis 1:14, which states that God appointed the sun and moon for "seasons, and for days, and years."

3. Others ask, "Are the six days mentioned in Genesis 1 days of twenty-four hours, or long periods of time?" Much has been

said on both sides. In this connection let us remember three things:

First, in these two chapters the word *day* is used in several senses. In 1:5*a*, 16, and 18 only the light part of the period is called day, as we now speak of the daytime. In the last part of verse 5 and also in verses 8, 13, 19, 23, and 31 the evening and the morning together are called day, and in 2:4 the whole period of creation is spoken of as a day.

Second, God, being God, could have done the whole work of the six days in six seconds, if He had so willed.

Third, if the six days are long periods of time, or if they are days of twenty-four hours, there is nothing in the account to contradict either view.

4. Keep in mind the prominent truth of these first two chapters of Genesis, that man was the crowning creation of God, and that he was made *like* god—in God's image. It is difficult for us to conceive what unfallen Adam was like. In heaven, when we shall be "like" Christ, our experience will bring enlightened knowledge.

So the first man was not a low being, striving to survive through the vicissitudes of an evolutionary process. He was a crowning creation in the image of his Creator.

Lesson 3

The Fall

Everything about chapters 1 and 2 of Genesis is bright, glorious, and promising. All the creations of God were good; the environment into which Adam was placed was perfect; the union of Adam and Eve was blessed; chapter 2 ends on the note of a clean record, "not ashamed." What a contrast strikes the eye as one now begins to read into chapters 3 and 4. Here the record is a black one indeed, with the story of evil, darkness, shame, cursing, and woe.

Look at the chart of Genesis on page 14, and note that the second great subject of the book is the fall.

Before reading further in this lesson guide, follow these suggestions and attempt answers for the questions:
1. Read through the two chapters slowly and carefully. Become thoroughly acquainted with the sequence of events. Here again, as in the previous lesson, you will find it very helpful to record on a rectangular analytical chart the main content of the action paragraph by paragraph, using the following paragraph divisions: 3:1; 3:8; 3:14; 3:16; 3:17; 3:20; 3:22; 4:1; 4:8; 4:17; 4:25.
2. In what paragraphs of chapter 3 is God a main actor?

_____

Who are the main actors of the paragraph in 3:1-7?

_____

Make a study of the phrases in this paragraph using the name "God."

_____

_____

3. Notice the questions of God in 3:8-13. Make some present-day applications.

_____

_____

4. In your own words, write out the curses placed by God on each of the following:
serpent

_____

woman

_____

Adam

_____

5. What seem to be the main purposes of the record of chapter 4?

_____

_____

6. What do you learn about salvation from 4:6-7?

_____

_____

7. Compare 4:9-12 with the similar account in chapter 3.

_____

_____

8. What do you learn about sin from these chapters?

_____

_____

9. What do you learn about God from these chapters?

_____

_____

_____

10. What are the bright verses of these chapters?

_____

_____

I. THE TEMPTATION (3:1-7)

It is important for us to notice how our first parents fell, because the serpent's subtle enticement is representative of the plan by which Satan tempts every man. Our great enemy has no new devices to practice on this generation. He is using today the same wiles he has been using on the human family since its birth. These are recorded in the Bible, and if we know our Bible we may be prepared and fortified when he attacks us in a similar way.

By comparing Genesis 3:1 with Revelation 12:9 and 20:2 we see that this "serpent" was Satan taking the form of this "beast of the field."

Read the first six verses of chapter 3, and notice with what subtlety Satan dealt with Eve. He simply asked the apparently innocent question, "Hath God said?" but in that question he cast doubt upon God's word. That is just what the devil is doing today —casting doubt upon God's word and trying to get people to doubt that the Bible is the Word of God. He came to Eve in the form of a serpent. He comes to us very often in attractive form. The aim is the same, to fill the mind with doubt and uncertainty. Whenever doubt that the Bible is the Word of God enters the Christian's mind, he should recognize it as an attempt on Satan's part to get him to take the first downward step that leads to destruction.

In answering Satan's first questions, Eve incorrectly quoted God, making the command more severe and lightening the penalty. God had said nothing about "touching" the fruit, and He had warned of *immediate* death for violation ("in the day," 2:17).

Satan saw his advantage instantly, as he always does with one unfamiliar with God's Word; and his next bold step was to call God a liar—"Ye shall not surely die"—when God had said, "Thou shalt surely die." That is what Satan is doing today, denying the truth of God's Word. From beginning to end, the Bible teaches that the wages of sin is death, not only to the body but to the spirit and soul. But Satan is constantly whispering, in a thousand different ways, "Thou shalt not surely die," "God is too good to punish sin," "There is some way out," "Thou shalt not surely die."

In verse 5, Satan goes on to misrepresent God's character; and Eve listens and believes the devil's lie, instead of God's blessed truth, as many are doing today. And this, after all God had done for Eve and her husband, making them His representatives in this beautiful world and giving them dominion over everything!

But observe, Satan kept back a very important part of the truth—as he always does when he advises. He did not tell Eve that she "should know good without the power to do it, and evil without the power to resist it." He let her find that out by bitter experience. God tells us the truth, the whole truth, and nothing but the truth, although it is sometimes unpleasant to hear. Eve first listened to Satan, then believed him, then obeyed him, until (v. 6) "she took of the fruit thereof, and did eat, and gave also unto her husband with her; and he did eat." That is the death-knell of all their innocence. The *object* of Eve's (and therefore Adam's) moral test was a tree that to the senses was "good for food . . . pleasant to the eyes," and also "to be desired to make one wise." Her options were to (1) eat of the tree and disobey God, or (2) refuse the fruit, obeying God. Numbed by Satan to the imperative fulfillment of God's commands and judgments, she chose the first option, was joined by her husband, and both were immediately overtaken with the overwhelming sense of guilt (3:7). They tried to hide their guilt by a covering of fig leaves. As soon as sin is committed, how prone the human heart is to cover it rather than confess and forsake it! But any coverings for sin that we make—fair promises, good deeds, and excuses—are like the fig-leaf coverings; they do not satisfy even ourselves—much less God.

II. DEATH BY SIN (3:8-19)

The first dispensation ended in failure. (See chart p. 9.) The instant Adam and Eve partook of the fruit, they were lost sinners, separated from God by their sin. God's word had proved true. Spiritually they were "dead in trespasses and sins," for spiritual death is separation from God. They had cut themselves off from God, and the only way they could get back to Him now was through repentance and faith, as we shall see. Though Adam and Eve tried to hide from God's presence among the trees of the garden, they could not elude His pursuit. God fired His questions in rapid order. "Where art thou?" "Who told thee?" "Hast thou eaten of the tree?" "What is this that thou hast done?" Each answer was an attempt at self-justification. But God was not deceived. There were the guilty ones before Him—Adam, Eve, and the serpent. The judgment on the serpent was pronounced, but included in the judgment was hope for mankind in the prophecy that the Seed of the woman would bruise the serpent's head (3:15).

Verse 15 is the first prophecy of Christ, the first faint glimmer of the "bright and morning star." Dim as it was, it was enough to light Adam's pathway and save his soul. In this first prophecy of Christ, we are told at least three distinct things about the coming Deliverer of the race. He was to be born of the human race— "seed of the woman." He was to be bruised. He would conquer Satan—"bruise thy [the serpent's] head." The head is a vital part of

29

the body, the heel is not. In giving forth this prophecy, it is as though God had said to Adam and Eve, "You have by your own choice become lost sinners, but there is hope. By Him, the Seed of the woman, your enemy shall be conquered. Look to Him."

Then God pronounced the heavy penalty of travail on the woman and the man for their disobedience. And then it would seem that God withdrew, leaving the man and the woman alone amid all the wreck and ruin they had wrought by their folly. How shocked and bewildered they must have been over it all! How deeply they must have regretted ever listening to the tempter!

III. SALVATION BY FAITH (3:20-24)

Gradually "the light of faith began to steal over the countenance of Adam." He was likely reflecting over what God had been saying to the serpent, that the Seed of the woman should bruise his head. Would the seed of this woman standing by his side someday be able to overcome Satan and give them back the life they had forfeited? The name Adam gave his wife—"Eve" (Hebrew *Chavah*, meaning "living")—suggests that he entertained such a hope.

No sooner did Adam show this measure of faith in God's promise than God returned and clothed Adam and Eve with coats of skins (v. 21). It was as though God had said: "You are right in supposing you need a covering for sin; but the best you can make does not satisfy even yourselves, else you would not have hid when I called. I will make you a covering that will be entirely satisfactory, even to Me." It could very well be that God at this appropriate time showed Adam how to offer the body of the animal as a sacrifice, and explained that as the smoke thereof ascended heavenward, it spoke with force and beauty of the acceptableness of such an offering to the Father. We are not told anywhere in the Bible when this ceremony of sacrifice was instituted; but in the very next chapter we see Abel offering an acceptable offering in this way.

Clothed with the garments of skins, our first parents were sent from the Garden of Eden to their life of toil. Sons and daughters were born to them (5:4), but we are told the names of only three of their children. The sad history of the two eldest is given in the familiar story of chapter 4.

IV. THE FIRST SONS OF ADAM (4:1-26)

Notice that Adam's first son, Cain, followed the way of death by sin; Adam's second son, Abel, followed the way of salvation by faith. From that day to this, every man and woman has chosen one of these two paths.

Cain and Abel each brought an offering to the Lord. As we imagine the two altars before us, we see Cain's piled high with fruit and grain; on Abel's there are choice, fat, slain animals. The record tells us that God accepted Abel's offering but did not accept Cain's. What made the difference? The epistle to the Hebrews gives the answer, where we read, "By faith Abel offered unto God a more excellent sacrifice than Cain" (Heb. 11:4). Abel had a heart of faith in God, but Cain did not. To what extent the sacrifice itself reflected obedience to directions God may have given to the men is not clearly known. There is the suggestion of the works of faith, possibly obedience to ritual directions, in God's words in 4:7: "If thou *doest* well, shalt thou not be accepted?" Another suggestion is offered by the biblical text. As we compare the description of the two offerings, we note that Abel's offering was of the *best* that he had—the fattest firstlings of his flock—whereas Cain perhaps may not have brought his best, for the biblical description merely states his offering was "of the fruit of the ground." Whatever was the situation of the offerings themselves, we do know from Hebrews that Abel's offering was accepted because Abel's *heart* was one of *faith in God.*

Thus at the outset of the human race, God gives the story of these two sons of Adam to set before us the two classes of men in every age: those who give their lives to God in faith, and those who refuse to trust in Him. Beyond this, note the mercy of God in offering Cain an opportunity to change his heart and amend his ways (4:6-7). But Cain persisted in his sin, thereby inviting havoc to his life as he would let sin beget sin. He murdered his brother, lied to God, refused to repent, and was sent from the presence of God as a fugitive and vagabond in the world. Did his sin visit generations after him? Precisely so, as is borne out by the very next verses of the Genesis account (4:16-24), wherein are recorded Cain's marriage and the names of his descendants. (Concerning his marriage, it is obvious that Cain's wife was one of his sisters, she being a daughter of Adam [see 5:4-5]. The marriage of immediate relatives was unavoidable in the early stages of the race's propagation, for how else could the race propagate?) Other sins of the human race are described in the record of Cain's descendants. Lamech, husband of two wives, exulted in the fact that he had slain two men for wounding him and proudly asserted his determination to defend his action to the uttermost.

Having recorded the genealogical line of the murderer Cain up to a certain point, the Genesis account is now free, so to speak, to give the line of divine promise and purpose, that of Seth. The

31

birth of Seth is recorded at the end of chapter 4; the genealogical line is presented in chapter 5. Chapter 4 closes on the bright note that in the days of Seth and his son Enos men began to call upon the name of the Lord as they worshiped their Jehovah God—Covenant Maker and Covenant Fulfiller.

V. SOME THINGS TO OBSERVE

1. In Genesis 3:6 Eve was tempted in three ways: (1) by the lust of the flesh, "good for food"; (2) by the lust of the eyes, "pleasant to the eyes"; (3) by the pride of life, "to make one wise." Compare 1 John 2:16. Christ was tempted in these three ways (see Matt. 4:3-11). Eve altered God's word as she met Satan's temptation, and she fell (see 3:2-3); but Christ met Satan every time with a quotation from God's Word, and overcame. Satan is constantly tempting us in these three ways. Let us always meet him as did Christ, with the sword of the Spirit, which is the Word of God.

2. Genesis 3:9 shows that from the very first, God sought lost sinners.

3. Notice from 3:17-18 that thorns and thistles are the result of man's sin. The ground was cursed because of Adam.

4. The seventh man from Adam through the line of Cain was the boastful murderer Lamech, whereas the seventh man from Adam through the line of Seth, the human ancestor of Christ, was Enoch (5:1-22), the man who "walked with God" and did not see death.

5. As early as the time of Enoch, Christ's second coming was preached (see Jude 14-15).

SUMMARY

As we look back on these two chapters of Genesis, by way of summary, the following truths are seen to be given prominence (review in your own mind the details of the story behind each truth):

1. *The deceitful activity of Satan* against man, luring him away from God

2. *The righteous indictment of God* against sinful man, condemning him to just recompense

3. *The gracious provision of God* in sparing the life of the human race, to assure objects of future redemption

4. *The messianic promise of God* in the prospect of a coming Redeemer

5. *The ongoing propagation of the human race*, individuals choosing to exalt God or self

Lesson 4

The Flood;
Birth of Nations

In our last lesson we saw how, through man's disobedience, sin entered and blighted this fair earth; and we saw some of its fearful results. In this lesson we shall see sin's terrible culmination in God's judgment by a catastrophic flood, and in a later judgment, dispersion. Genesis 5 serves mainly in a connecting capacity by listing the generations of Adam through the Seth line up to Noah and his sons (vv. 29, 32), thereby identifying the main character of the Flood story that follows. Chapters 10 and 11 pick up the genealogy record again for the generations of the sons of Noah *after* the Flood (10:1). Your study questions for these latter two chapters will be given toward the close of this lesson. Concentrate now on chapters 5 through 9.

First, read chapters 5 through 9 in one sitting. Underline in your Bible, or record on paper, phrases that stand out. One of your observations in reading the Flood story will very likely be that the account is filled with many details even to the point of repeating different items. Here again, as in the case of the structure of the creation account, there is not a *multiple* record of the event, but *one* continuous description as told from various vantage points, in order to include various emphases. You will see this purpose very clearly if you will make up an analytical chart (as suggested in the earlier lessons) and record the main contents of each paragraph of the four chapters (6-9). Make your paragraph divisions at these points: 6:1; 6:8; 6:11; 6:14; 6:18; 7:6; 7:13; 7:17; 8:1; 8:6; 8:15; 8:20; 9:1; 9:8; 9:18. (Think of chaps. 6 through 9 as *one* continuous story, though you will have four blocks on the chart, one for each chapter.) In your own words write down the main point of each paragraph, noting how each paragraph introduces something new to the unfolding story of the Flood. When this has been recorded you will have a good grasp of the sequence of the descriptions and actions of the Flood story.

33

Now answer the following questions, referring to the biblical text for your answers:

1. Write out the names of the descendants of Adam, as given in 4:17-24 and 4:25–5:32. Compare the seventh from Adam through Cain with the seventh from Adam through Seth (as to what the Bible says about each).

2. What evidences from these chapters point to the continuation of the Edenic curse up to the time of Noah?

3. Chapter 6. Give the reasons for the contrasting statements "I will destroy" and "I will establish my covenant."

4. Why *seven* of certain creatures (7:1-5) for the ark? What later paragraph does this paragraph anticipate?

5. What are the stages of the Flood described by this story? What was the extent of the Flood's devastation?

6. Note the references to Noah's obedience to God's many commands.

7. What other good things are said of Noah's character? (Cf. 6:22; 7:1, 5; 8:20; Heb. 11:7.)

8. What was the sequence of events as Noah disembarked from the ark? (8:20–9:17).

9. What does 9:18-29 tell you about how long Noah lived after the Flood?

_____

_____

10. List three spiritual lessons that may be learned from the story of the Flood.

_____

_____

I. SETH'S DESCENDANTS (5:1-32)

In Genesis 4 we have the history of Adam's first two sons. Genesis 5 introduces us to another man, Seth, Adam's third son, whose descendants we read about all through the Old Testament. Christ came through the line of Seth. In this chapter Seth's descendants are traced down to Noah.

Notice the great age of the men who lived before the Flood. Nearly all named in this chapter lived more than nine hundred years.

Notice, by adding the ages of these men, that Noah's father was living when Adam died. Noah's father may have had many conversations with Adam.

Notice from Genesis 4:26 that the testimony to Jehovah was committed to the line of Seth and not to the godless line of Cain. "Then began men to call upon the name of the Lord."

II. THE FLOOD (6:1–7:24)

Population had increased greatly in the earth, likewise wickedness. The moral condition of humanity before the Flood can be seen by 6:1-2, 5, 12-13. As God looked into the hearts of men, He saw that they were utterly corrupt. But there was one man who had faith—Noah (see Heb. 11:7). Faith is never overlooked nor unrewarded by God. So this man, because of his faith, became God's confidant and prophet. God revealed to Noah that He would destroy all flesh by a flood of waters, and He directed this upright man to build a long, narrow ark, with the window in the top and the door at the side, to populate the ark with animals of every kind, and then to enter the ark with his family. When the rain came with all its fury and destructiveness, it could not touch Noah and his family, for they were safe within the ark. What a type of Christ we have in this three-storied ark, with its heavenward-

35

looking window! The deluge of God's wrath and judgment against sin broke over Christ and spent its fury upon Him; but we who are safe in Christ, shut in by God's own power, can never be touched by it. Though death and judgment rage all around us, in Christ we need not fear. In Him are life, safety, peace, light, and sustenance.

When God made this revelation of His will, Noah went forth to do two things—announce to the world the coming judgment, and build the ark. We can well imagine that while Noah worked on his ark—a project of years—he must have had to endure a great deal of jeering from the people. Whatever chills of terror the people may have felt when Noah first announced the Flood, these soon were dispelled as the days and weeks and months and years passed by, and no floods came. All things continued as usual. The skies were bright, the seasons returned in their appointed time, the earth yielded her increase. There was no indication of anything out of the ordinary coming to pass. And so, as is natural to the human heart, men depended upon appearances more than on the word of God; their fears were lulled to sleep, and they went on in their wickedness, growing worse and worse. But Noah believed God against them all, and one day the fearful rains broke upon the people in the midst of their revelry. Words are inadequate to depict the scene. As the windows of heaven were opened with a heavy rain, the fountains of the great deep were brought upon the lands. Slowly and surely, higher and higher, arose the awful flood, until all the high hills under the whole heaven were covered, and every living thing in the earth died except those in the ark.

What a solemn lesson the world should learn from this story of the Flood. In our day the conditions are much the same as before the Flood. As the population has exploded, so also has man's wickedness. Preachers of righteousness stand in their pulpits week after week, year after year, announcing, as did Noah, a fearful judgment that is coming—a certain and eternal death to all those outside the ark of safety, Christ Jesus. But the people will not believe, assuming that all things apparently will go on as usual. The skies are bright, the seasons return in their appointed time, research, invention, and knowledge are on the increase. But God's Word has announced a future coming judgment, and only those are secure who obey God's Word as Noah did.

III. AFTER THE FLOOD (8:1–9:29)

When the fearful flood was over, Noah and his family came out into a renewed and cleansed earth. When Noah left the ark he "owned" the earth. Notice what Genesis records as the first thing Noah did on disembarking from the ark: "Noah builded an altar unto the Lord," offering burnt offerings on it (8:20). As the acceptable sweet savor ascended heavenward, God promised never again to bring a like judgment upon the earth. This was the hour and day for a new beginning. A new dispensation was begun, under which man was placed under human as well as divine law—the Dispensation of Human Government (see chart, page 9). Man was now permitted to eat animal food, whereas before only grains and fruit were allowed (cf. 9:3 with 1:29). Man was instructed to avenge by death the sin of murder. Also the rainbow was given as the token of God's covenant never again to destroy all flesh by a flood.

IV. NATIONS (10:1–11:32)

We come now to the fourth great fact in the book of Genesis —the birth of nations, covering chapters 10 and 11. While the genealogical listings in chapter 10 give names of individuals, the intent of the record is to identify the geographical distribution of the peoples and nations that grew out of the sons of Noah after the Flood (10:5, 20, 31-32).

First read Genesis 10 and 11, underlining any words or phrases that stand out. Don't get bogged down in the genealogical listings; rather, in this first reading, note only names that seem familiar to you from your previous biblical knowledge. Now answer the following questions:

1. How is chapter 10 divided according to subject? Compare verses 5, 20, and 31. How is verse 32 a summary verse?

_____

_____

2. Note geographical phrases throughout the chapter that indicate one of the main purposes of this chapter.

_____

_____

3. Chapter 11. What was the language situation of the world before the building of the Babel tower?

_____

_____

4. What were the people's motives in building the tower?

_____

_____

5. What were God's reasons for His action?

_____

_____

6. Compare the genealogical list of 10:21 ff. and 11:10 ff. What is the point of the latter?

_____

_____

7. In what ways is 11:27-32 an introduction to chapter 12?

_____

_____

8. List some spiritual lessons you have learned from reading these chapters.

_____

_____

_____

The reason God divided men into nations is told in chapter 11, and the basis on which the division is made is told in chapter 10, and briefly stated in 9:18-19. In other words, the events of 11:1-9 were prior to the geographical distributions of chapter 10. By referring to a map of ancient geography (see *The New Unger's Bible Handbook*, p. 41) and looking for the names of the descendants of these three sons of Noah, you will observe that the descendants of Japheth went north and west, the descendants of Ham went south and west, and the descendants of Shem south and east. Although Genesis 10 has been much criticized and disputed, archaeology is confirming its record for the source of the earth's race.

Notice the first few verses of chapter 11, and see how self-centered men had become. Their motivation was twofold: to achieve power of unity ("lest we be scattered") and to achieve boastful status ("let us make us a name"). God saw the bud of rash defiance appearing and chose to nip it before it flowered to its ultimate proportions. By God's simply confusing their tongues so that they could not understand one another, the people were scattered abroad, and their self-centered plan shattered. With this dispersion, the Dispensation of Human Government closed.

By adding up the ages of the men in chapter 5 and in 11:10-32, we find that God has been dealing with the human race for at least two thousand years. During these two thousand years He had tried man under three different dispensations, and man had proved a failure under each one. At the building of the tower of Babel (11:4), we see "all mankind practically turning their backs upon God. His truth and name were likely to be lost to humanity." So now God selected one man, Abraham, and from him trained up a nation, which He chose to be a "repository of His truth, a channel through which the promised Seed of the woman, the Redeemer of the world, could be born and identified when He came," and a channel through which God's blessing should ultimately flow out to the whole world.

So the next two thousand years, from Abraham to Christ (see history chart, p. 8), was a period during which God dealt especially with this one nation, Israel.

SUMMARY

The Genesis chapters we have studied in this lesson record three basic facts of the early human race:

1. The human race continued to propagate itself to the proportion of the size of nations.

2. The evil of individual men grew to the proportion that impelled God to destroy all of mankind except a remnant.

3. The evil of the people as a whole, after the Flood, was punished by confusion and scattering before it could reach its ultimate proportions.

Lesson 5

Abraham—
Four Great Tests

We have just left that section of Genesis that deals with the human race as a whole, where not *persons* but *events* are predominant (refer to your survey chart of Genesis as a review and to get your bearing before you proceed to read any further in the text of Genesis). Now, chapters 12 through 50 tell the story of the family of Abraham, the people whom God called and raised up, and through whom He would reveal Himself to the world. The chapters tell the story of the four great patriarchs: Abraham, who was sovereignly chosen to be the father of the nation, his son Isaac, Isaac's son Jacob, and Jacob's son Joseph.

First read chapters 12 through 14 in one sitting. Then get ready to record some things on paper. Follow the procedure suggested in earlier lessons by making rectangular blocks on a separate sheet of paper (8 1/2″ x 11″) to represent each chapter or segment, and marking off the paragraphs in the blocks. For this study you will have three blocks, thus:

12:1–13:4	13:5-18	14
12:1 ABRAM'S CALL	13:5	14:1
4		
10		
17	14	13
		17
13:2		
4	18	24

Now reread the three chapters, paragraph by paragraph, recording on your chart in as few words as possible the gist of each paragraph (e.g., for 12:1 you might write, "Abram's call"). Get in the habit also of underlining key words or phrases in your Bible as you read along in the studies.

By now you will have a fair acquaintance with the continuity of the story of these three chapters. Feel free to record in your paragraph blocks any observations you have already made in the chapters. Especially look for thoughts or events that are similar in nature, or repeated. Seek also to evaluate the *actions* and *words* of Abraham as they are recorded in his biography. The following questions and suggestions should be worked out before reading further in the workbook:

1. Locate the paragraph where a blessing is given Abraham. What is involved in each blessing? Mark your paragraph blocks to show this study.

2. Which of the blessings of 12:2-3 is a prophecy of Christ?

_____

3. On your chart mark places where Abraham erected altars or worshiped God.

4. One major purpose of these chapters is to relate the tests of Abraham's heart and character, and how he responded to them. Identify 4 major tests, as to what each was testing, and Abraham's response in each case. Record this study also on your chart.

5. Was any truth in the statement that Abraham tells Sarai to make in 12:13 (cf. 20:2, 12)?

_____

6. Make a study of the steps in Lot's backsliding (13:10-12; 14:12).

_____

7. Compare the words and actions of the two kings that met Abraham (kings of Salem and Sodom; 14:17-21).

_____

8. It will be helpful to fix in your mind the geography of Abraham's life, following his movements from place to place. On the map provided (p. 48-49), draw lines representing those movements for this lesson and for the lessons to come.

The preeminence of the redemption story in Abraham's history is shown by the large space given to it in the inspired volume

—nearly fourteen chapters. Only eleven chapters are given to record the history of the whole race for the two thousand years previous. It is as though God would hasten over those first two thousand years, as important as their events were, to relate in detail the beginnings of the redemptive story. Surely, as we shall see later, the history of this nation descended from Abraham is of the utmost importance for us to know and understand. Bear in mind that the Bible is not so much the history of man as it is the *history of the redemption of man*.

Abraham was the great man of faith. Faith and obedience were the two grand principles that controlled his life. It is well worth one's while to become intimately acquainted with this man whom God called His friend.

Our study will center about the four great tests that God gave Abraham.

I. THE TEST OF OBEDIENCE (12:1-9)

Abraham (or Abram as he was then called) was living in Ur of the Chaldees when he received God's call to forsake all and follow Him into a new land that He would show him (v. 1). Chaldea in Abram's day was a land of idols and idol worshipers, materially wealthy, and culturally advanced. When one considers what Abram was being called away from (a good land, friends and kindred, an established dwelling) and what he was called to (an unknown land, pioneering, arduous journeyings), one can appreciate the intensity of the test God was giving him. But in the call God also gave Abram great and precious promises (vv. 2-3), many of which have already been fulfilled. God gives every sinner a similar call to forsake his idols and self-life, and to come out into a new life with God. Together with the call, God gives exceeding great and precious promises, all of which He is ready to fulfill. The land to which God called Abram, the land of Canaan, or Palestine, is in some respects the most important spot on the earth's surface. It is here that most of the events recorded in the Bible occurred, and it is here that the Son of God passed the thirty-three years of His life in the flesh. This land was selected by God as the very best in which to train the nation, a nation that was to be His channel of blessing and the repository of His truth. Canaan is a type of the life into which we are called in Christ.

Verses 4 to 9 describe Abram's steps of obedience in answer to God's call. The key phrase is "so Abram departed, *as the Lord had spoken unto him*" (v. 4). Notice how definitely Abram related God to his life by the altars he set up. Trace his journeys on your map. Notice the reference to Lot, Abram's nephew. Lot was to have much to do with Abram's life in Canaan. The two represent two classes of people who respond to the call of God and come into the Christian life. Abram represents the spiritually-minded, increasing in wisdom, growing in grace, following on to know the Lord. Lot represents those who believe and are justified (2 Pet. 2:7-8) and are therefore saved from death, but who nevertheless want to hold onto the things of this world, its pleasures and attractions—the worldly-minded. Watch the careers of these two men, and see why Abram's is the exemplary one.

II. THE TEST OF TRUST (12:10–13:5)

"And there was a famine in the land" (v. 10). While it is true that famines were not uncommon in Abram's day, especially in the South or Negeb region of Canaan to which Abram for some reason had journeyed (v. 9), this famine apparently was the test of Abram's trust in God for His providence at such a time. (Cf. God's later words to Isaac under similar circumstances, 26:1-2.) Without any command from God, Abram went "down" into Egypt (v. 10) and got into trouble. (Trace on map these movements of Abram.)

Approaching Egypt, Abram again showed his failing trust in God's protection by manufacturing a half-lie (still a lie!) to insure his own life (vv. 10-16). But his sin was found out; he failed this test. God plagued Pharaoh, and Pharaoh expelled Abram and his company from Egypt.

Abram knew how to secure God's favor again—humbly repent and seek the face of God at the altar of consecration. And so he returned to Bethel "unto the place of the altar, which he had made there at the first: and there Abram called on the name of the Lord" (13:4).

III. THE TEST OF VALUES (13:5-18)

This test arose out of a normal development. Abram and Lot had been dwelling together, but the substance (cattle, flocks, etc.) of each had grown to such proportions that strife arose between the herdmen of each. Abram valued peace and suggested a "partitioning" of the land. Abram also valued ways of selflessness and, though it was his right to have the first option, he gave Lot that right. Lot displayed a greedy sense of value, choosing the well-watered plains of Jordan for his cattle. This was the first step down for Lot, for it caused him to pitch his tent toward the city of Sodom and then to move into that corrupt city (14:12). When he first came to the city he may not have known what kind of people lived there; but when he found he had got into such a crowd as that

(13), instead of leaving, or staying there and preaching righteousness, we see him settling down among them, sitting at the gate of Sodom, allowing his daughters to marry the men of Sodom, and apparently not lifting his voice against their sin.

Deep down in Abram's heart was the faith that the God who promised He would bless Abram would really do so. This is what Abram valued, and his trust was confirmed when God renewed the promise of the land and seed (13:14-17). Lot chose for himself; God chose for Abram. Who got the most? Even from a material standpoint, Abram was ahead. In one moment more real estate was deeded to him than Lot possessed in all his life; and from a spiritual standpoint, Abram was one of the richest men who ever walked this earth. It pays to let God do our choosing. Abram's gratefulness to God is seen in his erecting another altar of worship, at Hebron.

IV. THE TESTS OF LOVE AND LOYALTY (14:1-24)

Abram knew that God's promises were not to him alone but to his family and people, and to generations yet to be born. He loved his people, and even though Lot had gone his own way, associating with the sinners at Sodom, Abram loved Lot also. He was intent, therefore, on protecting his family and the land from intrusion by any foes. One day a messenger from Sodom ran into Hebron with tidings of war. Four Eastern kings had come over and again conquered five kings of the country of Canaan, including the king of Sodom, and Lot was among the captives. The invaders had fled in the direction of Damascus. Abram waited to hear no more. He must rescue Lot. So, taking his 318 trained servants, he pursued, overtook them near Damascus, surprised them by a night attack, rescued Lot and the other prisoners and the goods, then turned homeward. On reaching the vicinity of Jerusalem he was met by two kings: the king of Sodom and the king of Salem. The king of Salem, Melchizedek, was also a priest of God, serving some God-fearing group over whom he ruled. The significance of his words was that he recognized Abram to be "of the most high God," and that he blessed God for giving Abram deliverance from the enemy. The king of Sodom, to show his gratefulness to Abram, offered Abram the spoils of the battle, which Abram politely refused. Abram would not have it said that an outsider had made him rich. His loyalty was to God, who had promised him all riches.

The events of chapter 14 served favorably in behalf of the young nation of God's choosing. Abram had demonstrated within his own family a heart of love. And he and his people had demonstrated to the nations round about that God was their God and their blesser and their strength.

SUMMARY

Make a list of spiritual lessons you have learned from these three chapters.

_____

_____

_____

_____

What qualities of Abram's character helped to make him the friend of God?

_____

_____

_____

Lesson 6

Abraham's God of Promise

In these chapters the promise originally given Abram is restated, amplified, and symbolized for the benefit of Abram. From 15:1 to 18:15 the covenant itself is predominant, appearing over and over again in the text. From 18:16 to the end of chapter 20, events are related that show some of God's ways with the land that He promised in the covenant.

I. GOD OF THE COVENANT (15:1–18:15)

For this study block out three rectangles, with the suggested paragraph divisions: Block 1 (chap. 15): paragraphs at verses 1, 7, 12, 17; Block 2 (chap. 16): 1, 7, 15; Block 3 (17:1–18:15): 17:1, 9, 15, 22; 18:1. First, read the three sections in your Bible, noting places where God repeated or added to the covenant promise. Write on your charts, briefly, the substance of each paragraph of each of the three segments. Answer the study questions, referring to the text for your answers. Record things as you go along.

A. *God's covenant assured* (chap. 15). In the first paragraph (1-6), what is Abraham's question?

_____

Relate it to one word in verse 1.

_____

What is the one main promise of verse 5?

_____

What sign did God point to as a measure of this promise?

_____

Notice Abram's reaction. Read Romans 4:1-3; Galatians 3:6; James 2:23.

Now notice the item promised in the second paragraph (7-11). What question did Abram ask when he heard this promise?

_____ .

Abram in effect was requesting a sign. Study verses 9 to 17 in search of the sign God gave him. Then notice that God described the geography of that promised land (18-21). Relate these verses to verse 7.

_____

_____

After Abram carried out God's instructions for the covenant ratification ceremony (9-10), God gave him a vision (12-16) in which He mapped out the history of Abram's descendants for several hundred years. It is a most remarkable prophecy, every detail of which has been exactly fulfilled. The Egyptian bondage (13), the judgment on Egypt (14), the Exodus (14), and the possession of Canaan (16) were all revealed to Abram before he even had a child!

B. *Abram's impatience* (chap. 16). In this chapter we see the impatience of unbelief, the folly of not quietly waiting for God to bring about His promises in His own way and in His own good time.

First, read the entire chapter. Then compare verse 1*a* with verse 15*a*. Was Abram's problem really solved?

_____

Did Abram really have a problem?

_____

What was his mistake?

_____

What do you learn about God from verses 7 to 14?

_____

_____

Abram made the mistake of acting upon the suggestion of his wife without inquiring of God. They attempted to hasten the promises of the Almighty by their own devices. But this led only to unhappiness and strife. For thirteen years the slave girl and her son were disturbing elements in that otherwise peaceful home. However, God overruled all this to His glory, giving Hagar a son, Ishmael (lit. "God shall hear"), whose seed would be many, and

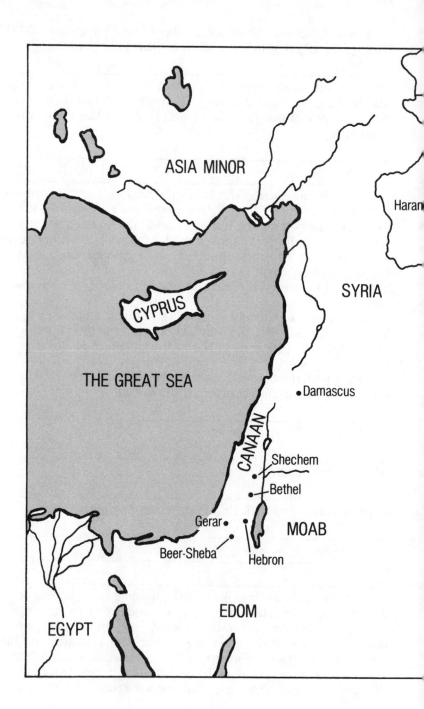

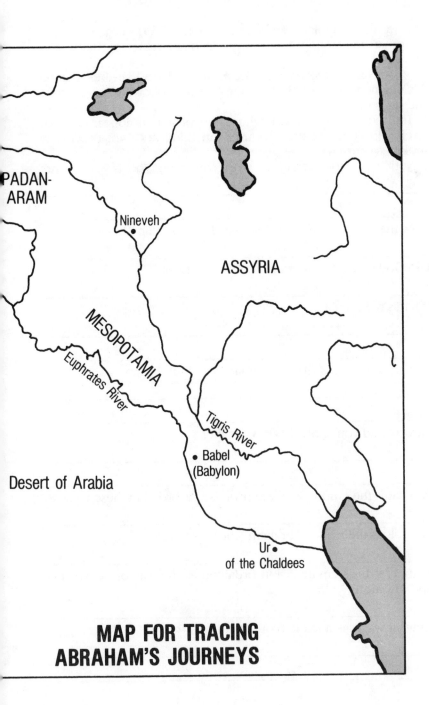

PADAN-
ARAM

Nineveh

ASSYRIA

MESOPOTAMIA

Euphrates River

Tigris River

• Babel
(Babylon)

Desert of Arabia

Ur •
of the Chaldees

**MAP FOR TRACING
ABRAHAM'S JOURNEYS**

who would be the father of a great nation (17:20). (Read Gal. 4:22-31 for an interesting NT application of the story of Hagar and Sarai.)

    C. Abram enters into the Covenant (17:1–18:15). After reading this segment in your Bible, complete the following suggestions and questions.

1. Indicate on your chart where the promises appear. Record briefly the items of the promises. Anything here not previously spoken to Abram?

2. Notice the repetition of the word *covenant*. What is a covenant?

_____

_____

How many parties are needed to make a covenant?

_____

Did God say "our covenant" or "my covenant"?

_____

What is the point?

_____

_____

3. In 17:1-8 what is God's command to Abram?

_____

_____

How would you apply this to your life?

_____

_____

4. What is the emphasis of the promise recorded in these verses?

_____

What does the name "Abraham" mean? (margin)

_____

5. In 17:9-14 is circumcision ordained as the way of deliverance and salvation?

_____

In what way was it a token of the covenant? (17:11)

_____

_____

Was Abraham forced to enter into this covenant?

What verses tell of Abraham's response?

6. Read 17:15-21. What items of the promise are recorded here?

What does the name "Sarah" mean? (margin)

Relate to each other the new names of Abraham and Sarah.

7. See 18:1-15. In what verse do you have the first clue as to the reason for the visit of the three men?

What was their question?

Who is the key character of verses 9-15?

Had Sarah heard this promise firsthand before?

8. Apply 18:14 to your own life. Look for other spiritual applications from this section. List them here.

SUMMARY (15:1–18:15)

When God spoke to Abram about an exceeding great reward, Abram was encouraged to ask, "What wilt thou give me?" God's answer was clear and unequivocal, though of fantastic proportions: He would give Abram numberless seed, many nations, and an extensive land. So great was that promise that Abram and his wife Sarai sinned in two different ways over it. First, they could

51

not bear to wait to see its fulfillment, so attempted to assist God by making Abram a father by Sarai's maid. Second, they could not believe a child could come of them in their old age, and so laughed at the promise. But God in His grace and long-suffering did not cast them off nor annul the promise. Of Ishmael, Abram's son by Sarai's maid, God promised a great nation, and God invited Abram to active participation in *His* covenant by the symbol of circumcision. The words "I will be their God" (17:8) accurately reveal the sovereign initiative of God to be Israel's Saviour.

II. GOD OF THE LAND (18:16–20:18)

These chapters tell of some of the immediate problems or situations that faced Abraham concerning people who dwelt in the land, and of God's disposition in each case. A good way to identify the essential facts of these chapters is to see what each teaches about Abraham, God, Lot, and the land. Record your findings thus:

SEGMENT	ABRAHAM	GOD	LOT	THE LAND
18:16-33				
Chap. 19				
Chap. 20				

1. Compare the faith of Abraham of 18:15-33 with that of chapter 20.

_____

_____

2. What truth about God's judgment should Abraham have learned from the long intercessory conversation with God?

_____

In chapter 14 Abram delivers Lot by effort. By what does he deliver him now (chap. 18)?

_____

3. Why do you suppose Lot's sons-in-law refused his warnings?

_____

According to chapter 19, what kind of a man had Lot become?

_____

What does this tell you about Abraham's heart?

_____

Of God's heart?

_____

4. What do verses 37 and 38 suggest as to how Lot's sin would later affect Israel?

_____

5. Though Abraham's conduct in chapter 20 does not honor his high calling, what is he still (20:7)?

_____

_____

What does this tell you about God?

_____

What important lesson is to be learned for Christian living (cf. Phil. 1:27)?

_____

_____

Three men appeared to Abraham sitting in his tent's door (18:1-2), and two angels appeared to Lot sitting in the gate of Sodom (19:1). The accounts of the two meetings present a bold contrast of character. Abraham represents the spiritual believer and Lot the worldly believer. After Abraham had been told again that Sarah would bear a son (18:1-15), the visitors left to deliver a message to Lot also, and Abraham accompanied them on their way toward Sodom. Presently one of the three, the Lord Himself, stopped, and began to talk with Abraham. Abraham was God's *friend*: God "whispered" His secrets to him. The wickedness of Sodom had reached such a climax that God must destroy the city and all the inhabitants. Immediately Abraham thought of his kinsman Lot and began to plead for the city of his dwelling, Sodom.

Once before he had saved Lot by effort. Now he saved him by intercession. God promised to spare the whole city if even ten righteous persons could be found; and at this the conversation ceased. What God was really telling Abraham was that judgment would fall on *individuals* for their individual sin.

Chapter 19 has to do mainly with the history of Lot. Only two angels came to Sodom (v. 1). They found Lot sitting in the gate of the city and at first declined his invitation to spend the night in his home. After some persuasion, however, they entered, and then the wicked men of Sodom surrounded the house. From the little we are told of them (vv. 4-9), we see they had fallen to such depths of iniquity that God's decision regarding them was just and wise. Sodom had become a plague-spot of sin, which could not be allowed to spread if the earth was to be saved from corruption such as prevailed before the Flood. God owns this earth and has a right to "eject bad tenants" whenever He sees fit.

The message that the angels delivered to Lot was a great contrast to the one they delivered to Abraham, which filled all the place with joy. They had only a message of doom for Lot. They told him that the next day the place was to be destroyed and that if he had any relatives he must go out and warn them to escape. So Lot went to his sons-in-law and urged them to save themselves while there was yet time; but he had not the slightest influence on them—and we cannot wonder. He had made his dwelling among the Sodomites all those years, and though his soul had been tormented day after day with their lawless deeds (2 Pet. 2:7-8), he had done little of a positive nature to bring them to repentance for their sin. And now when he suddenly began talking about judgment and death and being saved, they could not believe he was serious, and he failed to persuade a single one to leave. How important for God's children today to bear a clear, positive witness of the gospel in order to influence lost souls.

Lot himself seemed loath to leave Sodom, although he knew it was doomed. In the morning he "lingered," and the angels had to drag him and his family out of the city, "the Lord being merciful unto him" (16). And even when he was safely out, and the angels urged him to escape to the mountain (17), note how he talked (18-20). His heart was set on a "city." He was not willing to break the ties of his former ways and move on in faith to a new experience. The mountaintop of faith on which Abraham dwelt was an altitude altogether too high for such a man as Lot. Some Christians talk as Lot did when they are urged to take a stand, by faith, on new and high ground. They plead to hold onto some pet sin or worldly pleasure, small as it may seem. They are unwilling, as was Lot, to cut off everything that pertains to the old life of sin. But absolute surrender is what God desires.

Observe the end of Lot's career in contrast to that of Abraham's. Lot became the father of the Ammonites and the Moabites, who were in future years among the worst enemies of the chosen race, retarding their progress whenever possible. Lot himself was saved, but the influences for which he was responsible were to retard and hinder the progress of God's people. In contrast, see the end of Abraham's career. Throughout his life he glorified God, and now, after four thousand years, his name still is great among Jews, Christians, and Muslims. Through him Christ was born, and all families of the earth have been blessed.

There is a similar contrast between the influence of a spiritual Christian and that of a worldly one. A worldly Christian may be saved himself, but the influences for which he is responsible retard and hinder the progress of Christ's kingdom; whereas the spiritual Christian is not only a blessing in his life but his influence lives after him and blesses many.

One more event in Abraham's life is recorded in the Genesis account before the birth of Isaac. It is a regrettable event, but it teaches much about God and human nature. God instructed Abraham to move about in the land (20:13), apparently with the view to gradually settling his people in it. God promised always to be with Abraham, but it was over this that Abraham doubted, hence his agreement with Sarah to lie for protection. Sojourning in Gerar, the test case arose with Abimelech, king of Gerar. The lie was told, but God intervened and nipped the flower in its bud, mercifully renewed the ministry of Abraham His prophet, judged Abimelech for sin but restored him, and gave an opening to Abraham to dwell in Abimelech's territory (20:15). Abraham, though sadder for the experience, was learning more of God's sovereign testing ways concerning a chosen people and a promised land.

RECAPITULATION (15:1–20:18)

These chapters concerning Abraham's God of promise have pointed to great lessons learned by Abraham. Some of the highlights are:

1. *Sign of the covenant*—God's covenant, initiated by Him, but entered into by Abraham, by agreeing to the sign of circumcision.

2. *Seed through a miracle*—"Is anything too hard for the Lord?"

3. *Settlement in the land*—full appropriation was a long way off, but Abraham was seeing God's ways with the land.

4. *Sin under judgment*—"brimstone and fire from the Lord out of heaven."

5. *Sovereignty of God*—over His chosen people, His prophet Abraham, and nations of the world.

Abraham's Last Crucial Years; Isaac

The chapters of this lesson record some of Abraham's deepest experiences and introduce us to the son born in his old age.

ABRAHAM (21:1–25:18)

First read 21:1–25:18 in one sitting, underlining phrases that stand out to you. (This section offers a good number of such phrases from which spiritual applications may be derived.) Then block out on a sheet of paper (8 1/2" x 11" held sideways) five rectangles (as you have for previous lessons), labeling them by chapters, marking off paragraphs, and writing out the suggested titles (or your own), thus:

CHAP. 21 FULFILLMENT TIME	CHAP. 22 SUPREME TEST	CHAP. 23 BURIAL TRACT	CHAP. 24 FINAL TASK	25:1-18 LIFE'S TERMINATION
1	1	1	1	1
	9		10	
8		3	15	7
	15		50	
22	20	17	52	12
			62	
34	24	20	67	18

Now jot down in each paragraph box a word or short phrase identifying the content of the paragraph, and you will have an excellent visual pattern of the narrative of these chapters. Notice the intensity or gravity of each of Abraham's experiences. Study your charts further, and write out any additional observations (comparisons, progressions, repetitions, etc.) that you make. Now follow these further instructions:

1. The opening paragraph is 21:1-7 (Isaac born). Observe how this event determines the remainder of the narrative up to Abraham's death.

2. Who is the central figure of these chapters?

_____

What do you learn about Abraham here? List your findings.

_____

_____

_____

3. What does the section 21:22-34 add to the story of Abraham?

_____

_____

4. Why is 22:20-24 included? (Cf. 22:23 and 24:15.)

5. For what reason did God promise to make a nation of the descendants of Ishmael (21:13)?

_____

_____

What would this do for Abraham?

_____

_____

6. By what different names or titles had God been revealed to Abraham? (See 12:1; 14:18-19; 15:2; 17:1; 21:33.)

_____

_____

_____

_____

7. Describe Abraham's faith in chapter 22.

_____

Read also Hebrews 11:17-19. What about your faith?

8. What was the reason God gave for confirming His covenant by a sure oath (22:15-18)?

_____

9. What was Abraham's concern regarding the choice of a wife for Isaac (24:3)?

_____

Should Christian parents have a similar concern (2 Cor. 6:13-18)?

_____

10. Be able to tell the story associated with each of the following verses. Also make your own applications from these. This is excellent material for devotional talks.

a. "And the Lord did . . . as he had spoken" (21:21).
b. "And she . . . wept. And God heard the voice of the lad" (21:16-17).
c. "God is with thee in all that thou doest" (21:22).
d. "God did tempt [prove] Abraham" (22:1).
e. "Take now thy son, thine only son . . . and offer him there" (22:2).
f. "My son, God will provide himself a lamb" (22:8).
g. "The Lord God of heaven, . . . he shall send his angel before thee" (24:7).
h. "I being in the way, the Lord led me" (24:27).
i. "I will not eat, until I have told mine errand" (24:33).
j. "The thing proceedeth from the Lord" (24:50).
k. "And Isaac went out to meditate in the field at the eventide" (24:63).

I. FULFILLMENT TIME (21:1-34)

God always keeps His promises, however purposefully delayed, and in this chapter we read of Isaac's being born. There was great rejoicing over the child's birth. But amid the feasting (v. 8), there was one discordant note, one thing that marred the pleasure of the mother. She saw thirteen-year-old Ishmael mocking. Filled with sudden fury, Sarah told Abraham that the bondwoman and her son must be cast out; Hagar's son should not be heir with Isaac. Abraham's reaction was one of grief; and though, because

God instructed him to do so, he must fulfill Sarah's wishes by casting these out, he was assured again by God not only of the seed blessing through Isaac but that God would make a nation of Ishmael. God gave Hagar this latter message in her moment of despair in the wilderness. In this experience Abraham's tender heart with respect to his own family was clearly revealed. The story of the last half of the chapter reveals the testimony of Abraham's loyalty to God, which he maintained among the pagan nations dwelling around him, as seen in Abimelech's words: "God is with thee in all that thou doest" (v. 22), and in his permission to journey through those lands.

II. SUPREME TEST (22:1-24)

Of the early childhood of Isaac we know nothing. The action of this chapter took place when he probably was a young teenager. It was the occasion of Abraham's supreme test. Severe as this test was, Abraham's faith was equal to it. Here God seemed to contradict Himself. He had promised Abraham that from Isaac He would raise up a great nation; and then He commanded Abraham to offer Isaac as a burnt offering. How God would reconcile these two declarations Abraham did not know, nor was that his business. His business was to *obey* and leave the consequences with God. He had such implicit faith in God's word that he knew He would fulfill His promise even if He had to raise Isaac from the dead, which He did in a figure, as we told in Hebrews 11:17-19.

This incident in Abraham's life is full of instruction for God's children today. We should ever love the Giver more than the gift—be ready at any time to lay our all upon the altar, having implicit faith in God to work for our greatest good.

III. BURIAL TRACT (23:1-20)

In this scene Abraham was a mourner, seeking a burying place for his beloved and beautiful wife. He chose the cave of Machpelah, near Hebron, and insisted on paying for it. God had promised to give him the land, and he would not take a foot of it as a gift from the inhabitants of the land, even as he refused to be enriched by the king of Sodom.

Mark well the resting-place of Sarah. In this cave six ancestors of Christ were buried—Abraham and his wife, Isaac and his wife, and Jacob and his wife Leah—as though they were holding in trust the land that God had promised to give to their descendants. The mosque of Hebron stands on what is believed to be the site of this sepulcher and has been guarded for many years by the Muslims.

IV. FINAL TASK (24:1-67)

This is the last recorded business relating to the seed-promise that Abraham accomplished before his death. Nearing the end of his life, he wanted to be assured that Isaac would not take a wife of the Canaanites, so he sent his trusted servant to select a bride from among his own kindred in Mesopotamia. The servant, guided by God through a series of unique experiences, was eventually led to Rebekah's home, and when the matter of marriage was laid before her, she was perfectly willing to go as Isaac's bride. As she and her servant neared Abraham's home, Isaac himself came to meet her, "and she became his wife; and he loved her" (v. 67).

Many Bible students have seen in this exquisite story a picture of God the Father's sending the Holy Spirit into the world to gather a bride, the church, for His only Son, Jesus Christ. And in Isaac coming forth to meet the bride, Christ is seen coming forth from heaven when the church is caught up "to meet the Lord in the air" (1 Thess. 4:16-17).

V. LIFE'S TERMINATION (25:1-18)

To some, the end of life is death in every sense of the word, but to one who has lived for God, allowing faith and obedience to be the two grand principles of his life, the end is only an entrance into life more abundant; it is indeed glorification. God gave Abraham 175 years of life on earth, and when Abraham breathed his last breath he was "full" not only of years (as the King James Version implies in italics) but of experiences, of trials and temptations, of failures and victories, of walking with God as His friend, assured at the end of it all that he was God's, and God was his, and that God's great promises of blessing through his seed would surely come to pass. Thus Abraham was "gathered unto his people," while his sons Isaac and Ishmael, united in a common grief, buried him in the cave of Machpelah.

ISAAC (25:19–26:35)

There is comparatively little written of Isaac. Although he was living during the period described in chapters 21 to 36, Abraham and Jacob are the chief characters seen in these chapters. Only in chapter 26 is Isaac the main actor. But Isaac was a strong spiritual link in the chain of the earliest patriarchs, and the Genesis story bears this out. The proverb of the apple not falling far from the tree is surely true of Isaac, for in a sense his life was a duplicate of Abraham's. After Abraham's death, God's blessing on His people continued, but through Isaac (25:11). His wife, Rebekah, was barren, and Isaac entreated the Lord for a child as Abraham did, and was given two children, Esau and Jacob (25:21-26). Isaac, like Abraham, experienced famine in the land, but was explicitly told by God to remain in Canaan, where God would bless him. It was at this time that God's promises to Abraham were confirmed to Isaac. He obeyed God, and was materially blessed a hundredfold (26:12). His experiences with Abimelech, king of the Philistines, were also similar to those that Abraham had with the Abimelech of his day: representing his wife as a sister, having problems over herdmen, making a covenant of peace. Through it all, Isaac maintained a good testimony for God, so that Abimelech had to say of Isaac, "Thou art now the blessed of the Lord" (26:29). Chapter 26 could be called the miniature life of Abraham as seen in his son Isaac.

Isaac was a good man, and his prayerfulness and submission to God's will commended the blessings of God's faithfulness. He received God's covenant promises as being given for Abraham's obedience; he recognized them, benefited from them, and passed them on to his son Jacob.

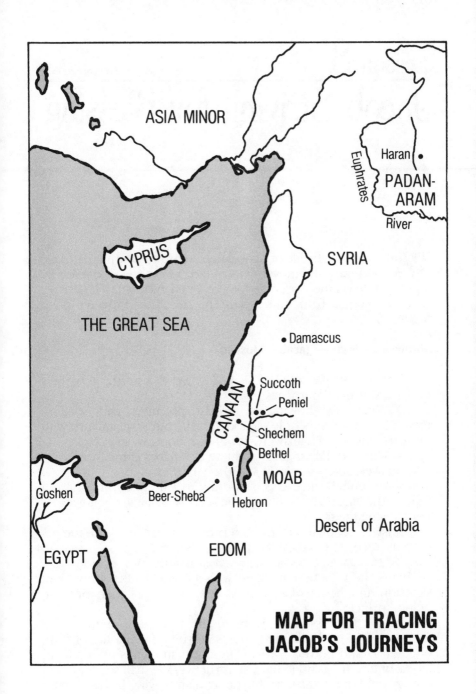

ASIA MINOR

Haran •
Euphrates
PADAN-
ARAM
River

SYRIA

CYPRUS

THE GREAT SEA

• Damascus

CANAAN

Succoth
Peniel
Shechem
Bethel

MOAB

Goshen
Beer-Sheba
Hebron

Desert of Arabia

EGYPT
EDOM

**MAP FOR TRACING
JACOB'S JOURNEYS**

Lesson 8

Jacob Striving for Blessing

While studying the life of Jacob, keep before you the map on page 63, and trace the movements of Jacob from place to place by a pencil line on the map. The four main characters of Genesis 12 through 50 are four names which you should always keep together:

Abraham — Isaac — Jacob — Joseph

The greater part of Genesis is devoted to a portrayal of their lives for two main purposes:

1. *Historical:* showing the origins, promises, and development of the chosen people of God, Israel. Your acquaintance with this early history will answer a lot of questions, such as:

—Where did the names of the twelve tribes come from?

Answer: See Genesis 29:31–30:24; 35:18.

—Do unbelieving Jews, returning to Palestine today, have a right to the land? Who really are the seed of Abraham, believing or unbelieving Jews?

Answer: Study the many land promises that God gave the patriarchs, recorded in these chapters of Genesis.

2. *Spiritual lessons:* the "ensamples" that Paul writes of in 1 Corinthians 10:11. Genesis is filled with spiritual truths about God, salvation, and the life of a believer. Keep your eyes open for these helpful principles.

In our last lesson we were meditating upon Abraham, the friend of God, and saw the benefits accruing from a life of faith, obedience, and prayer. A very different man comes before us in Jacob, but his life is nonetheless instructive. We shall see how God can lay hold of a selfish, willful, faulty man striving by his own efforts to gain material blessing, and so work in him that in the end his character is grand and beautiful, because he has repented and seen the true value and way of divine blessing.

In Abraham's life, God as initiator of a saving covenant is brought prominently before us. In Jacob's life it is God in His manifold grace. Grace is unmerited favor. It was by the grace of God, not by human merit, that Jacob became what he was at the close of his life.

First, read 25:19-34 and chapters 27 to 30. At the beginning of your study of Genesis you secured chapter titles for all the chapters of Genesis. Now is the time to review, amplify, and revise if necessary that cursory study with respect to the chapters of Jacob's life. Make the following familiar survey chart, filling in the *segment* titles now for the chapters of this lesson (27-30). (You will notice we said "segment" titles. This is because some units in the Bible are either longer or shorter than the length of the chapter, the chapter division obscuring the continuity of the text. Notice that three of the segments begin at verses other than verse one: 28:10; 29:31; 30:25.)

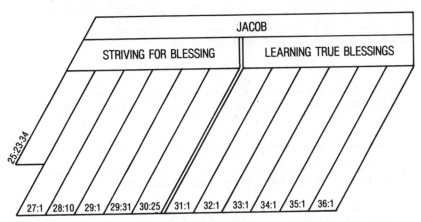

1. Study the chapters of this lesson with a view to seeing how Jacob foolishly and without faith strove to gain the blessing. Write down things he so did.

_____

_____

_____

_____

2. What was God's prophecy of the relationship of Esau to Jacob (25:23)?

_____

Was God able to fulfill His own prophecy?

_____

Did Esau have to sell his birthright so that God's prophecy could be fulfilled?

_____

3. In chapter 27 compare the blessings that Isaac gave to his two sons.

_____

_____

_____

4. Why did Rebekah want Jacob to flee to Haran? (27:42-45)

_____

_____

What reason did she give to Isaac? (27:46)

_____

_____

5. Compare Isaac's blessing on Jacob (28:3-4) with the Lord's promises to Jacob (28:13-15).

_____

_____

6. Did Jacob's ladder experience touch his heart?

_____

Evaluate the details of his vow (28:20-22).

_____

Did Jacob see deeper than material things?

_____

_____

7. The name "Jacob" means what (27:36)?

_____

Compare Laban's and Jacob's trickery as seen in chapters 29 and 30.

_____

8. 29:31–30:34. What do you learn about Leah, Rachel, and Jacob from these verses?

_____

_____

What may be learned about God from 29:31 and 30:22?

_____

From these verses what may be learned about childbearing?

_____

About husband-wife relationships?

_____

About the ways of God?

_____

In answer to the latter question, compare 29:31 and 30:22.

_____

9. Give the names of Jacob's twelve sons in the order of their birth.

_____

_____

_____

_____

_____

10. Who was the mother of Judah, through whom Christ came (29:35)?

_____

11. What was the final outcome of Jacob's relations with Laban as recorded in 30:25-43?

_____

_____

12. List five good lessons learned from these chapters.

_____

_____

_____

_____

_____

_____

BIRTHRIGHT (25:23-34)

After the birth of Jacob and Esau is recorded, their early years are described in these few words: "and the boys grew" (25:27). They bargained over Esau's birthright in their manhood years.

Isaac, living at Beersheba (see map), had doubtless carefully taught his two boys all that God has promised to Abraham (12:1-2 and 15:13-21), but they regarded the teaching very differently. These blessings of the future did not appeal to Esau. He was concerned entirely with the present life. He preferred to gratify his present needs and desires at the cost of future blessedness and so was willing to sell his birthright for a mess of pottage (vv. 33-34). Either he did not believe, or he did not value God's promises.

BLESSING (27:1–28:9)

The years passed on. Isaac, then old and blind, wished to give the blessing to Esau, his favorite son. However, before the boys were born, God had said, "The elder [Esau] shall serve the younger" (25:23). Rebekah, determined that her favorite son, Jacob, should receive the blessing, planned a cunning deception (vv. 6-17). Jacob acted a lie in being dressed to represent Esau; then he told a direct lie (v. 19). Note how pious he pretended to be while deceiving his blind old father (v. 20).

Although it was God's will that Jacob should receive the blessing and covenant promise of Abraham, He would have brought it about without all this maneuvering and deceit, and without interference on the part of Rebekah. Her efforts only made trouble. Esau, infuriated at losing the blessing, declared he would kill Jacob. In desperation Rebekah sent Jacob away to her brother, Laban, who lived at Haran, after first obtaining Isaac's permission, by intimating that she was afraid Jacob would marry one of the daughters of Heth. Rebekah had her way, but what was the result? She never saw her favorite son again so far as we have any record, and she sent Jacob out to more than twenty years of hardship. This was her recompense for managing instead of seeking God's guidance.

Jacob tried to buy the birthright and steal the blessing, and he may have congratulated himself on his shrewdness; but in future years he learned that his efforts were fruitless. Privileges and blessings are free gifts from God, just as the heavenly birthright and the divine blessing must ever be received as free gifts from God, not obtained by human effort.

LADDER (28:10-22)

So vivid is the picture, one can almost see Jacob hurrying away from his angry brother, fleeing from Beersheba toward Haran. (Trace on map.) Weary with a day's travel, he threw himself down to sleep, with nothing but a stone for a pillow. (Draw line on map to Bethel.) Jacob was a man so full of his own plans that God had difficulty in getting him quiet enough to reveal His plan for his life. God had a wonderful plan for Jacob, just as He has for every one of us. When Jacob was quiet in sleep, God opened heaven and disclosed His plan. From the top of the ladder (a type of Christ, the only medium through which our prayers can ascend and God's blessings descend) God talked with him (vv. 13-15).

What a marvelous future God stretched out before Jacob. How God heaped up the promises, both spiritual and material. But poor Jacob seemed able to grasp and comprehend only the material ones, as seen in his vow to God (vv. 20-21). Providing him enough to eat and wear and keeping him in safety were all Jacob could realize God was able to do for him. Very small in comparison to what God has said He would do! When God opened that dazzling prospect before Jacob, one would think he would at that time have surrendered himself entirely to God's leading. Jacob's experience at Bethel opened his eyes to some extent, but he still had a long way to go. Later on, God would remind him of this vow (31:13). For the time, at least, Jacob was content to regard the experience simply as an event in his life as he hurried on in his self-chosen way. Not until twenty years later did he surrender to God.

This Bethel occurrence is the first of two great crises in Jacob's life. According to God's gracious promise (v. 15), He never left Jacob nor forsook him until He had done all He had promised for him. God is ever the same. When one trusts God's promises, though he may makes many mistakes, God will never leave him nor forsake him until He has accomplished all He has promised —conformity to the image of His Son.

JACOB AND LABAN (29:1-30)

After a long journey, Jacob reached Haran (see map) and found his relatives, with whom he remained twenty years or more. His uncle Laban was in many ways similar to Jacob in character: both were bargain makers, deceivers, and liars. Instead of enjoying each other's society, they seemed bent on seeing which could outwit the other. Laban deceived Jacob in the matter of Leah and Rachel. Chapters 30 and 31 record how subsequently Jacob got the advantage over Laban in regard to the flocks and herds; how Laban changed Jacob's wages ten times; and so on—first one and then the other. Of course Jacob was seeking a wife at Haran (while fleeing Esau), but little did he anticipate the woes his search would bring him, including the problem of having two wives. Under God's judgment he was to reap what he had sown, before he would be in the place where God could restore the blessing of fellowship with Himself.

INCREASE OF CHILDREN (29:31–30:24);
OF WEALTH (30:25-43)

Both of these segments record the bright subject of increase and enlargement, but the accounts are dimmed by the unhappy circumstances involved. As to increase of family, twelve sons and one daughter were born to Jacob, but the feeling between his two wives, Rachel and Leah, was intense. Notice that Leah was the mother of Judah, through whom Christ came. She, not Rachel, was buried with Jacob in the ancestral tomb at Hebron. God compensated the unloved wife.

As to increases of possessions, these came to Jacob despite the arrangement of cattle and flocks that normally would have favored Laban. Unquestionably it was God's design to bring this great increase to Jacob, for the time had arrived for God to send him back to Canaan (cf. 31:3). It must be said of Jacob that during all these years at Haran, he had not forgotten God. Indeed, he attributed his business success to Him and paid Him a tithe of his increase. But, like many of God's children, he was so self-strong and self-resourceful that he was pursuing his own plans regardless of the plan God had for him. The Father's only resource with such children seems to be to put them where they *must* have His help—where they will be made to feel the *need* of God. Jacob soon was to be brought into such a place, as we shall see in the following chapters.

Lesson 9

Jacob Learning True Blessing

Our last lesson left Jacob at Haran, prosperous, worshiping God but not entirely surrendered to Him. Jacob had not been made to feel his dependence upon God. In this lesson Jacob comes to know God in a new way.

Read each chapter of this lesson carefully and prayerfully, absorbing the important lessons that God would teach you.

First, notice how the story begins (31:3) and how it ends (37:1). As you study these chapters, or segments, you will want to see what transpires in between. Briefly stated, this is a story of Jacob's immediate problems, of their solutions, and of his finally seeing who he really was and then surrendering completely to God.

Go back now to the individual segments, and record in the following boxes the main points of each. You may want to adapt or expand this method of studying. The following pattern should prove helpful.

JACOB REDIRECTED

31:1

16

71

JACOB'S PROBLEMS

WITH LABAN	WITH ESAU	WITH HIMSELF		WITH SURROUNDING NATIONS
31:17	32:1	32:22	33:1	33:18
55	21	32	17	34:31

.... (see at 33:1 Box) ....

(See 35:1)

↑
OUTCOME

RENEWED BLESSING

35:1
15

SOME CONCLUDING ITEMS

36:16
37:1

1. Record in the three boxes where God met and spoke to Jacob. What did Jacob learn and receive from God in each experience? Make a thorough study of this, because these are the clues to Jacob's final discovery of spiritual success, and therefore are important for your own edification.

2. Reread 31:1-16. Notice the contrasts at these places: verses 2 and 3; 5a and 5b; 7a and 7b; 9a and 9b. Record these. What did Jacob learn?

_____

_____

What do you learn of Jacob from verse 11?

_____

Why did God remind Jacob of his former vow (v. 13)?

_____

_____

What about vows and decisions made by Christians today?

_____

3. In 31:17-55 what is Jacob's problem?

_____

_____

How was he protected by God?

_____

_____

Compare Jacob's confidence of verses 36-42 with his earlier fear (31-32).

_____

_____

Compare Laban's early anger (23-36) with his later submission (43-53).

_____

_____

How do you account for the changes? Was the cairn (heap of stones) of Mizpah a testimony of faith or an admission of cunning (49-50)?

_____

_____

4. Read 32:1–33:17. What was Jacob's problem concerning Esau (3-4)?

_____

_____

What was Jacob's first wise move (5)?

_____

_____

What three things did Jacob do on hearing of Esau's approach?

_____

What do you learn of Jacob from his prayer?

_____

Notice the elements of adoration, confession, thanksgiving, and supplication in this prayer. What are your reactions on reading chapter 33?

_____

_____

5. According to 32:22-32, what is the meaning of the name Jacob?

_____

Of Jacob's new name?

_____

Of Peniel?

_____

Did Jacob obtain power with God when he was strong or when he was weak?

_____

In resistance or submission to God?

_____

6. What is Jacob's problem in 33:18–34:31? (v. 30)

_____

Notice where Jacob had settled down (33:18). What was God's solution to the problem (35:1)?

_____

_____

7. Read 35:1-15. What spiritual lessons do you learn from these verses?

_____

_____

_____

8. Do you think the death of Isaac may have been delayed by God for any reason (35:27-29)? Explain.

_____

_____

_____

JACOB'S PROBLEMS (31:1–33:17)

When God told Jacob, "Return unto the land of thy fathers" (31:3), Jacob's mind flashed to two problems: Laban and Esau —how to leave the former peacefully, and how to face the latter safely.

The solution of the Laban problem developed gradually. First, Jacob had a sure commission and promise of help from God (31:3-13). Then, Jacob had encouragement from his wives (31:14-16). And God kept Laban from doing harm (31:24, 29). Jacob was convinced of his innocence (31:36), which gave him courage to deliver an ultimatum to Laban (31:36-42). The outcome was a covenant (31:44) and an amiable parting of the ways.

Before the Esau problem could be solved, Jacob needed to undergo a spiritual transformation, and this is the reason for his Peniel experience before actually meeting Esau.

Picture Esau with 400 men. Naturally Jacob felt uneasy about Esau. Years before, Esau had threatened to kill his brother, who now supposed that he intended to carry out his threat. Jacob's company, with the women and children, flocks and herds, would be no match for Esau's trained warriors, probably reckless and wild like himself. Jacob must have God's help. He began to realize that the time had come when he needed more than his own efforts or cunning. He made what preparation he could, and then threw himself on God. His prayer was a model one (32:9-12). But even though he sought God's help at this time, he did not *surrender* to God—not until after that night of wrestling.

At Peniel (see map) the second crisis in Jacob's life was reached. Genesis 32:24 marks the turning point in Jacob's career. His problem here was *himself*. The text poignantly says, "And Jacob was left alone." He was never the same afterward. Read verse 24, and note that it was the angel wrestling with Jacob at first (apparently the angel taking the offensive); and the angel's object seemed to be to break down Jacob's self-strength and show him what an impotent creature he was in himself—that he could gain nothing worth having by his own efforts but must receive all as a *gift* from God. But Jacob's self-life was very strong, and so, all through the long hours of the night, the two wrestled on, Jacob refusing to yield. At the break of day, the angel saw he had not prevailed, so he "touched" the hollow of Jacob's thigh and threw it out of joint. Then Jacob wrestled with the angel in prayer (25*b*). When Jacob pleaded for blessing, the angel asked, "What is thy name?" Humbly Jacob confessed it: "Jacob [supplanter]." In a word he confessed his true character. Instantly the angel gave him a new name: "Israel [prince]." Notice, he was not a prince in his own strength, but in his weakness. He prevailed only when his strength was broken and he humbly confessed his true character. Jacob was not allowed to go over into the Promised Land and inherit the covenant promises of Abraham until "with his self-strength broken down, and in humble confession of his true character-name, he hung helplessly upon God for the birthright which he had tried to buy, and the blessing which he had tried to steal."

Jacob's fears about Esau were groundless. Esau had no intention of harming Jacob but came with gifts and a welcome. God had appeased the wrath of Esau long ago. How God smooths the way before His children and removes the obstacles to their progress! How easily tears of reconciliation flow when God melts human hearts!

FROM SHECHEM TO BETHEL (33:18–35:29)

Shechem was not God's place for Jacob to settle down. God apparently allowed the experiences of chapter 34 to make Jacob willing to leave the area of the foreigners. In this incident Jacob was disgraced by his children. Shechem's outrage of Jacob's daughter first brought disgrace upon the family, and afterward Jacob's sons heaped sin upon sin by their dishonest dealings with Shechem and his men. Of course, they had great provocation for anger; nevertheless, their dealings were dishonest. We cannot wonder at Jacob's sons being dishonest when we consider the history of their father and their mother, their grandmother and their uncle Laban, for children are very close observers and apt imitators. Jacob learned with great thoroughness the truth that "whatsoever a man soweth, that shall he also reap." He had sowed the wind; he reaped the whirlwind. He had deceived *his* father; his sons deceived him in a much more horrible way. These sons, from this time forward, almost broke their old father's heart by their wicked ways.

God then moved to extricate Jacob from his plight by ordering him to go up to Bethel. Jacob had been away for more than twenty years, but now he must get *back to the place where he first met God* and begin anew. Those twenty years, while he had been out of God's plan and place for him, were wasted years. How much better it would have been if he had surrendered to God at the first. Now he cleansed his house of idols (v. 2) and went up to Bethel. Genesis 35:1-15 is the bright record of a man restored to fellowship with God by His grace. Jacob's heart was further mellowed by the loss of his beloved wife Rachel. He moved on to Hebron, where his father, Isaac, was still living. If Isaac had died while Jacob was at Haran, God would have been left without a chief witness or representative in the Promised Land. So Isaac lived on until Jacob returned with his self-strength broken down and a new name given him. Having cleansed his house and heart of idols, Jacob was ready to take up the full Abrahamic testimony. Isaac passed from the scene of action, his lifework accomplished, and was buried in the cave of Machpelah by his two sons.

LAST YEARS OF JACOB'S LIFE

Chapter 36 simply tells the generations of Esau and of his going to Mount Seir from Canaan and from his brother Jacob. It gives the generation of Seir the Horite and the names of the kings of Edom before the time of the first king of the children of Israel.

The story of the life of Jacob does not end here. Beginning with the next chapter, Joseph becomes the prominent character, but we do see occasional glimpses of Jacob. These glimpses show us that he was steadily growing in grace, and when at last he did come to the end of his life, we see what kind of a man God had made of him. In Genesis 46 we see him blessing Joseph's children with very clear spiritual vision, although his natural vision was dim, as was his father Isaac's. Without the slightest hesitation he gave the *younger* son the chief blessing. This is the third instance in Genesis of the second son rather than the firstborn receiving the chief blessing. In chapter 47 we see Jacob humbly confessing to Pharaoh that his days have been "few and evil." Then in chapter 49, just before Jacob's death, we see him with his twelve sons gathered around him for blessing. God lifted the veil that usually hides the future from mortal eyes, and Jacob looked on through the centuries and saw clearly what should come to pass in years to come. In the calm elevation of faith, he bestowed the blessings "with a consciousness of power which only close companionship with God could possibly impart." His faith was like Abraham's, and his prophetic vision was keener than that of either Abraham or Isaac.

One writer has beautifully said that Jacob's life reminds one of a day in which the early hours are filled with clouds and mists and rain and wind, making it very disagreeable, but at the close there is a glorious sunset and a calm, peaceful twilight. The early years of Jacob's life were filled with clouds of unbelief, cunning, bargain making, and deceit; but at the close these were all swept away like mists. After a glorious sunset, in the calm, peaceful twilight Jacob serenely passed to the God he had at last come to know intimately.

SUMMARY

The highlights of chapters 31 through 36 are the three times when Jacob had an experience with God. At Haran, he was redirected by God (31:1-16). At Peniel he was broken and restored by God (32:22-32). At Bethel he was reassured by God (35:1-15). What would Jacob have been but for the grace of God! What would we be but for that same grace! Meditate over the spiritual lessons you have learned from these chapters of Genesis.

Lesson 10

Joseph as Prisoner

Joseph is one of the most beautiful characters in the Bible. His life should be studied for a twofold purpose: first, to imitate his virtues, and, second, to observe how remarkably he typifies Christ. The fact that Joseph maintained a good testimony in surroundings of sin and impurity teaches that it is possible for any believer to live a holy, godly life. The secret is to have the Lord as a constant companion, as did Joseph. Joseph was a model young man in every particular—true to his God, true to himself, true to his employers; a dutiful tender son; a kind, forgiving brother; a sympathetic, helpful friend; a strong, wise, businessman.

God's providence is wonderfully seen in Joseph's life. God was behind the scenes, so to speak, "managing all the springs of the vast machine of circumstance." The most likely and the most unlikely events were made to minister to the development of God's purpose for His chosen nation. Remember what God's purpose for His chosen nation was. He revealed it to Abraham (Gen. 15:13-14). Observe how naturally this began to be brought about in Joseph's life. Because of space limitation, this study guide can only point to the highlights of Joseph's experiences. You are encouraged to take the questions and comments as starting points and to develop substantial studies within each chapter. In the closing lesson of this guide appears a list of ways in which Joseph's life foreshadowed that of Christ.

First, read chapters 37 through 50 to get an overview of this large section of Genesis. Record chapter titles on the following chart.

Look for groupings of chapters according to content. Your divisions and wording may vary from those of the accompanying chart.

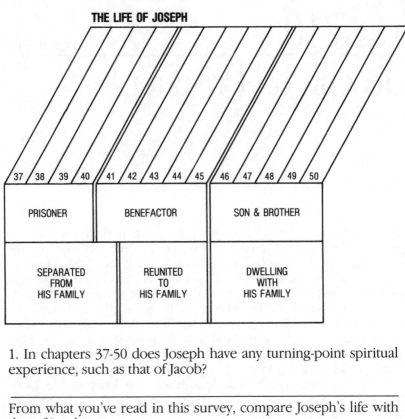

THE LIFE OF JOSEPH

| 37 | 38 | 39 | 40 | 41 | 42 | 43 | 44 | 45 | 46 | 47 | 48 | 49 | 50 |

PRISONER	BENEFACTOR	SON & BROTHER
SEPARATED FROM HIS FAMILY	REUNITED TO HIS FAMILY	DWELLING WITH HIS FAMILY

1. In chapters 37-50 does Joseph have any turning-point spiritual experience, such as that of Jacob?

_____

From what you've read in this survey, compare Joseph's life with that of Jacob.

_____

_____

_____

What is the key experience of Jacob in these chapters?

_____

2. Considering chapters 37-40, name five things you learned about Joseph's character.

_____

_____

_____

_____

How do you account for the favor Joseph enjoyed in his experiences?

_____

Why was there opposition against such a good man?

_____

What spiritual qualities did Joseph manifest under trial?

_____

3. Joseph does not appear in chapter 38 at all. Why is this chapter included in the record? (Keep in mind that Judah was one of the human ancestors of Christ.)

_____

4. Give two other reasons besides the one given in 37:3 for believing that Jacob may have loved Joseph more than his other sons.

_____

_____

5. Reread chapter 37. Why was Joseph unpopular with his brothers?

_____

_____

Did Joseph act wisely in the way in which he informed his brothers of his future favor?

_____

_____

Jacob, the supplanter of earlier years, now was the deceived one. What law does this illustrate?

_____

_____

List the kinds of sins mentioned in this chapter.

_____

_____

6. In chapter 39 what is Joseph's secret of victory in severe temptation?

_____

_____

Compare the beginning and ending of this chapter.

_____

_____

7. What one statement made by Joseph in chapter 40 reveals his relationship to God?

_____

_____

What lesson is learned from 40:23?

_____

_____

_____

JOSEPH SOLD (37:1-36)

Joseph came before us as a boy of seventeen, feeding his father's sheep, seeing visions of the future, and telling his brothers of his dreams of their obeisance. This excited the hatred of his brothers, as did the partiality that Jacob showed to his best-loved son and Joseph's testimony against their evil deeds.

The brothers went up to Shechem, and then still further from home, to Dothan. The father's heart yearned over his sinful children, and one day he sent Joseph out of Hebron (the place of fellowship) to inquire about the welfare of his brothers. When they saw him coming, they plotted against him and although Reuben wished to spare him, Judah sold him for twenty pieces of silver to a company of Ishmaelites from Gilead, who were going down into

Egypt to sell spices. Joseph's bloodstained coat, which they took to Jacob, convinced the father that Joseph was dead. Jacob refused to be comforted and felt that he had lost everything in life worth living for. But Joseph still lived and was sold to Potiphar, an officer of Pharaoh of Egypt.

JUDAH (38:1-20)

This chapter makes a break in the history of Joseph, to tell the story of Judah, through whose line Christ came. It seems to be introduced for the purpose of tracing the unbroken line of Christ (cf. Matt. 1:3). When one considers the men and women who were the human ancestors of Christ, one sees that He came to the very depths when He condescended to be made in the form of sinful man. Christ's perfect life could not possibly have been simply the outcome of a pure ancestry, as might have been claimed by some if all His ancestors had been like Abraham or Joseph.

JOSEPH IMPRISONED (39:1-23)

The key phrase of this chapter is "and the Lord was with Joseph" (39:2a). Notice how often this thought appears in the chapter.

The Lord was so manifestly with Joseph that people perceived that fact at once, as did Potiphar, who put all his business affairs in Joseph's hands. For some time all went well. But after a while Potiphar's unprincipled wife set her affections on this handsome young Hebrew, and because he stood true to the right she accused him of a crime he never even thought of committing, and had him cast into the Egyptian dungeon, which was a place of death. But God did not forsake Joseph in this time of adversity (see v. 21). That prison house, with the Lord as his companion, was a far brighter place to Joseph than the king's palace would have been with a guilty conscience. Joseph found the Lord's favor even in prison, because he determined not to sin against God: "How then can I do this great wickedness, and sin against God" (39:9).

JOSEPH INTERPRETS THE PRISONER'S DREAM (40:1-23)

Chapter 40 illustrates how God brings experiences to His children that ultimately bring about His good and perfect will in their lives. Joseph's contact with Pharaoh's butler and baker was not primarily for the servants' benefit but that one of them one day should remember what Joseph had done and thereby open the door to Joseph's favor with Pharaoh.

Up to this point in the account, the outlook for Joseph's release from prison was bleak. Doubtless he could not understand why these hard things had come into his life, for he was living as close to God as he knew how; but God had some purpose in it all, and Joseph trusted Him. Many dealings of God are not understood by His children at the time, but if they but continue to trust Him, He will make all things work together for good *to them*.

The butler and baker imprisoned by Pharaoh were especially sad one morning, and Joseph kindly made inquiry as to the cause. When they told him about their dreams, he immediately pointed them to God as the interpreter. This trait of Joseph's character is worthy of imitation. It matters not in what society he was placed, he was neither ashamed nor afraid to talk about his God. In his interview with that wicked woman he had talked about God (39:9). Here he directs his fellow prisoners to God (40:8). Later, when Joseph was brought before Pharaoh, the heathen king, the first sentence he uttered struck the keynote of his life—God (41:16); and even among the wicked members of his own family his testimony was clear (42:18). Not only by his life but by his words Joseph confessed God on all occasions.

Joseph interpreted the dreams of the butler and baker, and each of the dreams came true. The butler's life was spared, and he was restored to his butlership again; but strangely he forgot Joseph, and failed to intercede in his behalf. Joseph remained a prisoner for at least two more years. But God's timing was part of His design, and when God would have the butler remember Joseph, so it came to pass.

Lesson 11

Genesis 41–45

Joseph as Benefactor

In the last lesson we saw Joseph deprived of his liberty, his position, and his reputation—all because of his steadfast righteousness. It might appear from the standpoint of human reasoning that Joseph had made a mistake. But it is never a mistake to rigidly adhere to God's standards of righteousness. Rich rewards are for the righteous—always, though not necessarily immediately. In this lesson we see how Joseph was given far more than he gave up. It is always so. In fact, for Joseph there was the added blessing beyond *receiving* good things. He was made to be a *giver* of good things, a benefactor.

For your study, first read the chapters of the lesson. Then refer to your chart for the chapter titles. Think through the action of this part of the narrative. Note that the action takes place in Egypt, during Pharaoh's reign, over Pharaoh's grain, but Pharaoh is not a main character of the narrative except in the first forty-five verses of chapter 41. The main characters are: Joseph, his brothers, and Jacob. In your study find out first what each chapter reveals concerning these persons. Record your observations in the following chart:

CHARACTER REVEALED

CHAPTER	JOSEPH	HIS BRETHREN	JACOB
41			
42			
43			
44			
45			

The factor of *suspense* becomes predominant throughout the narrative of these chapters, the big question being when and how Joseph and his brothers and father will be reunited. This is significant in view of the fact that it was at least twenty-two years since Joseph had seen his family. Jacob sent his sons to Egypt to secure grain. Joseph recognized his brothers when first he saw them, but he hid his identity from them on purpose. Notice the things Joseph did or demanded while retaining his anonymity:

a. 42:15 _____

b. 42:19 _____

c. 42:25, 35 _____

d. 43:16, 18 _____

e. 43:29 _____

f. 44:2-5, 10 _____

Now read 45:1: "Then Joseph could not refrain himself..." The suspense was too much for Joseph. He must make himself known to his brothers. Chapter 45 cannot be read without emotion except by stony hearts.

Returning to each individual chapter, answer the following questions before reading further in the study guide:
1. In the section 41:14-36 note Joseph's numerous references to God. What do you learn about God from these verses?

_____

_____

_____

_____

About Joseph?

_____

_____

Was Joseph asked to give the advice of verses 34-36?

_____

_____

What should impel Christians to give advice (v. 38)?

_____

_____

In what sense was the Spirit of God in Joseph?

_____

_____

What is the Holy Spirit's relation to the Christian?

_____

_____

What do the names of Joseph's two sons reveal concerning his experiences in Egypt (vv. 50-52)?

_____

_____

_____

2. Why would Joseph want to hide his identity from his brothers as he did in chapter 42?

_____

_____

_____

Reconcile verses 7 and 24 as to Joseph's heart.

_____

_____

_____

What was the first testimony about God that Joseph left with his brothers (42:18)?

_____

_____

_____

What do you learn about a guilty conscience from this chapter?

_____

_____

_____

3. In chapters 43-44 what is commendable about the character of Judah, the ancestor of Christ (43:1-10; 44:14-34; cf. 49:8-12)?

_____

_____

_____

Deduce some lessons on intercession from Judah's pleadings.

_____

_____

_____

(Judah's plea of verses 16-34 has been described by Sir Walter Scott as "the most complete pattern of genuine natural eloquence extant in any language.")
4. What do you learn in chapter 45 about the free will of man and the sovereignty of God (4-13)?

_____

_____

_____

Note 45:15*b*: "And after that his brethren talked with him." What are some of the things you suppose they talked about?

_____

_____

_____

JOSEPH'S EXALTATION (41:1-57)

God's time had now come to release Joseph. Observe God's ways. He simply sent a dream to a heathen king (vv. 1-14). All the wise men of Egypt failing to interpret the dream, the butler was caused to remember the Hebrew in prison, and Joseph was sent for. Observe how Joseph never lost an opportunity to point people away from himself straight to God. In verses 15 and 16 Joseph has a fine opportunity to gain a reputation for himself, but instead he declines to take any personal credit and gives the glory to God. He told Pharaoh that in this drama God had shown what He was about to do. There were to be seven years of great plenty in Egypt, followed by seven years of famine. Joseph advised the king to set a man over the kingdom to gather the surplus grain in preparation for the coming famine. Pharaoh immediately selected Joseph, for the same reason that Potiphar had selected him as his business manager (see vv. 38-39). By the power of the king of the land, Joseph was lifted from the dungeon to a virtual throne and was given all authority in Egypt. Moreover, after his exaltation he was given a wife, the daughter of the priest of On (v. 45). During the next plenteous years, two sons were born—Manasseh and Ephraim. "And the seven yeas of dearth began to come, according as Joseph had said" (41:54). This was the attestation of the true prophet's message. Overnight Joseph found himself at the pinnacle of power. "And all countries came . . . to Joseph" (41:57).

FIRST VISIT OF JOSEPH'S BRETHREN (42:1-38)

Jacob, still living at Hebron, was alarmed because of the famine; hearing that there was grain in Egypt, he sent ten of his sons to buy a supply. He kept Benjamin, Rachel's youngest son, at home. Rachel was dead and Joseph gone; hence Jacob's heart twined around Benjamin—but even Benjamin was to be taken from him! God takes away our idols one by one. When the brothers met Governor Joseph of Egypt they did not recognize him. He had been only a lad of seventeen when they last had seen him. Now he was a man, almost forty, much changed in appearance, dressed in Egyptian costume, and speaking to them through an interpreter. Joseph recognized his brothers instantly, and as they bowed before him, he remembered the dreams of his youth and saw how God had fulfilled the promise then made. It is rather surprising, at first thought, to see the harsh way in which Joseph treated them (vv. 12-20). But this treatment was seemingly to awaken their conscience and bring them to repentance, which was the very effect it had (vv. 21-22). Why did they immediately think of Joseph? No one had mentioned the name. But how true to nature. When one gets into any difficulty, the mind flashes back to the unconfessed, unforgotten sin, and attributes present distress to past wickedness, as did these brothers!

SECOND VISIT OF JOSEPH'S BROTHERS (43:1-34)

Again Jacob's sons had to go into Egypt to buy grain. They told their father it was useless to go unless Benjamin accompanied them, as the lord of the country had declared that he would not even see them if they came without their youngest brother. Jacob objected; but at last, when Judah offered to stand surety for Benjamin's safe return, Jacob reluctantly consented. This time all went well; the governor seemed satisfied with their honesty and invited them to dinner. He seated them according to their age, showing wonderful insight into their past.

JUDAH'S PLEA (44:1-34)

Before the brothers had gone on their homeward way, they were overtaken by a messenger and accused of stealing the silver cup. Rightly they protested that they were innocent and suggested that search be made, that the one with whom the cup was found should die and that the rest be bondmen. The implanted cup was found in Benjamin's bag of grain. By their own agreement Benjamin, the very one whom they had promised to take back in safety to his father, was doomed to death, and all the rest were to be bondmen for life. There was nothing now but to throw themselves on the mercy of the governor. They were taken back to Joseph in deep humiliation. Judah's plea (vv. 18-34) "exceeds anything in literature, in pathos and simplicity." As he pictured the white-haired old father at home awaiting anxiously the return of his beloved son, and depicted the father's grief if Benjamin were not returned, it was too much for Joseph's loving heart.

As long as Joseph's brethren maintained their own righteousness, Joseph appeared to them to be stern and cruel and unreasonable; but when they came to him in deep humiliation, and threw themselves upon his *mercy*, he showed himself as their loving brother, with power to give them freedom and life.

IDENTIFICATION AND REUNION (45:1-28)

With what a start of surprise those brothers must have heard the words "I am Joseph, your brother, whom ye sold into Egypt" (v. 4). How they must have peered into his face to see if they could trace any resemblance to their long-lost brother.

Joseph evidently understood then the things that had seemed hard in his life. He recognized God's hand and purpose in all that had come to him (vv. 4-8). Also he used the opportunity of a lifetime to demonstrate genuine love by: (1) forgiving those who formerly wanted to slay him, (2) relieving their fears of vengeance, (3) weeping over seeing them again, (4) making arrangements with Pharaoh for his family's immigration to Egypt.

Joseph's direct contacts thus far had been only with his brothers. Yet his deepest love and concern were for his father. Not just for conversation did Joseph, after identifying himself, inquire first about his father: "I am Joseph; doth my father yet live?" (45:3). And when Jacob heard that Joseph was alive his spirit was revived, and he said, "I will go and see him before I die" (45:28).

Before leaving this lesson, go back over the narrative of these five chapters looking for the major spiritual applications. What is the best spiritual lesson you have learned here?

_____

_____

_____

What errors are there to avoid?

_____

_____

_____

What example is there to follow?

_____

_____

_____

Lesson 12

Genesis 46–50

Joseph as Son and Brother

In this lesson we finish the study of Joseph's life. Already we have seen to what heights of power and blessing God raises the one who lives true to Him and trusts Him, even though the way may be difficult and long.

Throughout the whole of Genesis, God is teaching the folly of not believing and obeying Him. Shall we learn these lessons and follow in the path God marks out for us?

Read carefully and prayerfully the chapters of this lesson. There is much food here for the nurture of the Christian.

For your study, refer to your segment titles on your chart after you have read through these chapters. Make any changes you desire to make at this time. You will find as you think through these six segments (five chapters) that there are three major units of subject matter, thus:

LAST DAYS OF JACOB & JOSEPH

	NEW HOME		FAREWELL BLESSINGS		DEATHS	
	46:1	46:31	47:29	49:1	49:28	50:15
JOSEPH ➔						
JACOB ➔						

In the blanks provided in the above chart, record what part Joseph and Jacob play in each segment, and you will have a good grasp of the narrative of these chapters. Record further studies on this chart as suggestions come to you along the way.

92

Now answer the following questions:
1. Where in these chapters are references made as to God's promises to Israel?

_____

_____

_____

Make a list of these promises.

_____

_____

_____

2. Why did God allow Jacob to go into Egypt (46:1-4) when He had commanded Isaac to stay in Canaan (26:1-5)?

_____

_____

3. Note how many of the house of Jacob came into Egypt (46:26-27). There is no discrepancy here. Joseph and his sons did not come "with Jacob." They were already in Egypt. Counting Jacob himself, there were exactly seventy.
4. Which son of Jacob took the leadership (46:28)?

_____

_____

5. How did Pharaoh treat the descendants of Abraham (45:17-20; 47:5-6)?

_____

_____

_____

6. How did Israel fare in the land of Goshen (47:27)?
7. What were the names of Joseph's sons (chap. 48)?

_____

_____

Which received the chief blessing?

_____

8. Make a study of Jacob's prophecies concerning his sons (chap. 49). To understand all the prophecies you will probably need the

93

help of a commentary. For your present study, look for spiritual lessons in the prophecies, especially in those concerning Judah and Joseph. List them:

Judah _____ **Joseph** _____

_____ _____

_____ _____

_____ _____

9. Compare the events attending the deaths of Jacob and Joseph.

_____

_____

_____

_____

10. How old was Jacob when he died (47:28)? _____

Joseph (50:22)? _____
11. Compare 47:29-31 with 50:25-26.

_____

_____

12. As a final review, list five lessons learned from the lives of each of the patriarchs:
Abraham

_____

_____

_____

_____

Isaac

_____

_____

_____

_____

_____

Jacob

_____

_____

_____

_____

Joseph

_____

_____

_____

_____

JOSEPH WELCOMES JACOB (46:1-30)

When Jacob's sons returned to him the second time from Egypt, they had strange news to tell—Joseph was alive and was governor of Egypt. Jacob could not believe it at first, but when he saw the gifts that Joseph had sent, and heard what his sons had to say, he was convinced. He decided to accept Joseph's invitation to spend the rest of his life in the land of plenty. His decision (45:28) was given God's approval and encouragement by a vision (46:2-4).

Notice that the seed of Abraham was now leaving Canaan. They would not see that country again until, some hundreds of years later after oppression in Egypt and trials of the wilderness, they would return under Joshua's leadership. Read Genesis 15:13-16 to see how these movements and events were foretold by God to Abraham many years previously, even before Isaac was born.

JOSEPH ENCOURAGES PHARAOH TO FAVOR JACOB
(46:31–47:27)

With the encouragement of Joseph, Pharaoh treated Jacob and his sons very generously. At the close of Jacob's life, he blessed Pharaoh (47:7). Recall that when God called Abraham from Ur of the Chaldees, one of the promises He made to him was "I will bless them that bless thee, and curse him that curseth thee." This test is put to _every_ nation. Thus far history has demonstrated that every nation that treats the seed of Abraham kindly is blessed, and every nation that treats them badly comes under a curse.

During the years of famine, Joseph first took money in exchange for grain. When the money failed, he took cattle. When all the cattle became Pharaoh's, Joseph took land in payment; and after that, the people offered *themselves* in payment for food. So Pharaoh, through Joseph, became absolute monarch, owning all the money, property, land, and people. Joseph took no credit to himself, but gave all the glory to the king.

But more important than the prosperity of Pharaoh was the blessing that Israel enjoyed in the land of Goshen. God was building up a large and fruitful nation in anticipation of later leading their succeeding generations back to the large land of Canaan.

"And Israel dwelt in the land of Egypt, in the country of Goshen; and they had possessions therein, and grew, and multiplied exceedingly" (47:27).

JACOB BLESSES JOSEPH'S SONS (47:28–48:22)

One reward Joseph received for his righteous life was to have his two sons, Ephraim and Manasseh, "adopted" by Jacob as his own sons (48:5), so that when the land of Canaan was later divided among the tribes, Joseph was represented by two full shares of territory. These verses record God's blessing on Jacob (48:3-4), on Joseph (48:15-16, 21-22), and on Ephraim and Manasseh (48:16, 20).

Joseph's younger son, Ephraim, received the chief blessing. This is the third time in Genesis that the second child rather than the firstborn received the chief blessing. Some take this to be a foreshadowing of the setting aside of Israel, God's "firstborn" (Ex.4:22), and giving the first place to the church of Christ.

JACOB BLESSES HIS SONS (49:1-27)

This was a solemn moment in Jacob's life, when he gathered together all his sons and spoke to each individually, prophesying blessings and cursings on their posterity in "coming days" (49:1, Berkeley Version). Some prophecies would find fulfillment in the tribes' inheritances of land parcels in Canaan (Josh. 13-19). Some had deeper and more distant implications, such as 49:10, which may have referred to the coming Messiah (and if so, this is the third prophecy of Christ in Genesis). Some of the highlights— good and bad—of the prophecies are indicated in the following list:
Reuben: unstable and not excelling (though endowed with strength and firstborn rights)

Simeon and Levi: to be scattered among Israel (in the land allotments, Simeon was absorbed in Judah, and Levites were given no land inheritance)

Judah: to be praised, to rule (through Judah the Messiah would come)

Zebulun: location of dwelling by the sea

Issachar: would submit to foreign invaders and become their slaves

Dan: would become a strong defender of Israel

Gad: a valiant overcomer in battle

Asher: to be prosperous in the produce of the field

Naphtali: would delight in freedom

Joseph: a prince among his brethren, but not without opposition; fruitful and victorious

Benjamin: to be feared in battle

JACOB AND JOSEPH DIE (49:28–50:26)

When Jacob had ended his farewell to his sons, he "yielded up the ghost, and was gathered unto his people" (49:33). Fulfilling his request to be buried in Canaan (49:29-32), Joseph organized a funeral entourage to carry Jacob's body to Canaan and bury it in the cave of the field of Machpelah. Back in Egypt, Joseph had another occasion to demonstrate his genuine love and forgiveness toward his brothers. He dispelled their fears of vengeance by speaking kindly to them with such promises as "I will nourish you, and your little ones" (50:21). Joseph remained a prince to the end! What a lesson in consistency! How noble a character!

And then Joseph died at the age of one hundred ten. In anticipation of one day fulfilling his request "carry up my bones from hence" (50:25), his brothers embalmed his body and placed it in a coffin in Egypt.

The book of Genesis thus closes with the death of one of its most noble characters. The greater part of Israel's history was yet to be written. Joseph's bones remained in Egypt but for a time. Gloriously God would bring His people out of Egypt by Moses; victoriously He would lead them into the Promised Land by Joshua. So the coffin awaited its removal, and a new day. And God was to prove Himself faithful in all His promises.

Before leaving this study of Genesis, consider Joseph as a type of Christ. Not every detail of Joseph's life was typical of Christ. Typology never requires this in any categories of type. Perhaps it may be said, however, that more types of Christ are found in Joseph than in any other biblical character. Here is a list of some of the prominent ones:

JOSEPH AS A TYPE OF CHRIST

Joseph	Jesus
1. Was the well-beloved son of his father (Gen. 37:3).	1. Was the well-beloved Son of His Father (Matt. 3:17).
2. Lived in Hebron, the place of fellowship, with his father before he was sent to his brothers (Gen. 37:14).	2. Lived in heaven, the place of fellowship, before coming to the earth (John 17:5).
3. His father sent him, and he was perfectly willing to go (Gen. 37:13).	3. His Father sent Him, and He was perfectly willing to go (John 3:16; Phil. 2:5-7).
4. Testified against his brothers' sin, and they hated him (Gen. 37:2).	4. Testified against men's sin, and they hated Him (John 15:18).
5. Revealed to them the exalted position he would hold in the future, and they hated him the more (Gen. 37:5).	5. Revealed to men the exalted position He would hold in the future, and they hated Him the more (Matt. 24:30-31).
6. His brothers plotted against him (Gen. 37:19-20).	6. His brothers according to the flesh (the Jews) plotted against Him (Luke 20:13-14; Luke 19:46-47).
7. Judah sold him for twenty pieces of silver (Gen. 37:26-28).	7. Judas sold Him for thirty pieces of silver (Matt. 26:15).
8. Was tempted and did not yield (Gen. 39).	8. Was tempted but did not yield (Matt 4:1-11).
9. Was accused wrongfully (Gen. 39:13-18).	9. Was accused wrongfully (Matt. 26:59-65).
10. Was put in the Egyptian dungeon, the place of death, with two malefactors (Gen. 39:20).	10. Was put on the cross, the place of death, with two malefactors (Mark 15:27-28).
11. One of the malefactors died and the other lived (Gen. 40:21-22).	11. One of the malefactors died and the other lived—spiritually (Luke 23:39-43).
12. Was raised from the place of death by the king of the land (Gen. 41:14).	12. Was raised from the place of death by the King of the universe (Eph. 1:19-20).
13. Was given all power in Egypt (Gen. 41:42-44).	13. Was given all power in heaven and earth (Matt. 28:18).
14. After his exaltation took Gentile bride to share his glory (Gen. 41:45).	14. After His exaltation takes Gentile bride (the church) to share His glory (Eph. 5:23-32).
15. Acknowledged to be the savior of the people and their ruler (Gen. 47:25).	15. Acknowledged to be Saviour and Ruler (Phil. 2:10-11).
16. All must get their bread (physical life) through Joseph (Gen. 41:55,57).	16. All must get spiritual life through Jesus Christ (Acts 4:12).
17. Gave all honer to the king and delivered all things into his hands (Gen. 47:14-20).	17. Gives all honor to the King (God) and delivers all things into His hands (1 Cor. 15:24).
18. Knew the history of his brothers (Gen. 43:33).	18. Knew what was in man (John 2:24-25; Matt. 9:4).
19. When his brothers humbled themselves before him and threw themselves on his mercy, he freely forgave them (Gen. 44:45).	19. All who confess their sins receive His forgiveness (1 John 1:9).

Bibliography

COMMENTARIES AND TOPICAL STUDIES

Alleman, H. *Old Testament Commentary*. Philadelphia: Muhlenberg, 1948.

Boice, James Montgomery. *Genesis: An Expositional Commentary*, 3 vols. Grand Rapids: Zondervan, 1987.

Erdman, Charles R. *The Book of Genesis*. Westwood, N.J.: Revell, 1950.

Kevan, E. F. "Genesis." In *The New Bible Commentary*, ed. F. Davidson. Grand Rapids: Eerdmans, 1963.

Leupold, H. C. *Exposition of Genesis*. Columbus: Wartburg, 1942.

Pfeiffer, Charles F. *The Book of Genesis*. Grand Rapids: Baker, 1958.

Pieters, Albertus. *Notes on Genesis*. Grand Rapids: Eerdmans, 1943.

Pink, Arthur W. *Gleanings in Genesis*. Chicago: Moody, 1922.

Thomas, William H. G. *Genesis: A Devotional Commentary*. Grand Rapids: Eerdmans, 1946.

Yates, Kyle M. "Genesis." In *The Wycliffe Bible Commentary*, ed. Charles F. Pfeiffer and Everett F. Harrison. Chicago: Moody, 1962.

RESOURCES FOR FURTHER STUDY

Clark, Robert Edward David. *The Universe: Plan or Accident?* Philadelphia: Muhlenberg, 1961.

David, John. *Paradise to Prison: Studies in Genesis*. Grand Rapids: Baker, 1975.

Dowley, Tim. *The Moody Guide to Bible Lands*. Chicago: Moody, 1987.

Jensen, Irving L. *Jensen's Survey of the Old Testament*. Chicago: Moody, 1978.

Klotz, John William. *Modern Science in the Christian Life*. St. Louis: Concordia, 1961.

Morris, Henry M. *Studies in Bible and Science*. Grand Rapids: Baker, 1966.

Nelson, Byron C. *After Its Kind*. Minneapolis: Augsburg, 1952.

New International Version Study Bible. Grand Rapids: Zondervan, 1985.

Payne, J. Barton. *An Outline of Hebrew History*. Grand Rapids: Baker, 1954.

Pfeiffer, Charles F., and Vos, Howard F. *Wycliffe Historical Geography of Bible Lands*. Chicago: Moody, 1967.

Ryrie Study Bible. Chicago: Moody, 1978.

Sauer, Erich. *The Dawn of World Redemption*. Grand Rapids: Eerdmans, 1953.

Schaeffer, Francis. *Genesis in Space and Time*. Downers Grove: InterVarsity, 1972.

Schultz, Samuel. *Old Testament Speaks*. New York: Harper, 1960.

Strong, James. *The Exhaustive Concordance of the Bible*. New York: Abingdon, 1890.

Tenney, Merrill C., ed. *The Zondervan Pictorial Bible Dictionary*. Grand Rapids: Zondervan, 1963.

Unger, Merrill F. *New Unger's Bible Dictionary*. Chicago: Moody, 1966.

Vos, Howard F. *Genesis and Archaeology*. Chicago: Moody, 1963.

Whitcomb, John C., and Morris, Henry M. *The Genesis Flood*. Philadelphia: Presby. & Ref., 1962.

Wood, Leon. *A Survey of Israel's History*. Grand Rapids: Zondervan, 1970.

Young, Edward J. *An Introduction to the Old Testament*. Grand Rapids: Eerdmans, 1949.

Zimmerman, Paul, ed. *Darwin, Evolution and Creation*. St. Louis: Concordia, 1959.